WONDERFUL WORLD OF KNOWLEDGE
YEAR BOOK 1982

Disney's

Wonderful
World of
Knowledge

YEAR BOOK 1982

GROLIER ENTERPRISES, INC.
Danbury, Connecticut

ROBERT B. CLARKE   *Publisher*

WILLIAM E. SHAPIRO   *Editor in Chief*

FERN L. MAMBERG   *Executive Editor*

MICHÈLE A. McLEAN   *Art Director*

RICHARD SHAW   *Production Manager, Manufacturing*

ALAN PHELPS   *Production Manager, Production*

. . . .

HOWARD B. GRAHAM   *Senior Vice-President, Publishing*

BERNARD S. CAYNE   *Vice-President and Editorial Director*

HARRIET RIPINSKY   *Vice-President and Director of Manufacturing*

ISBN 0-7172-8130-2
The Library of Congress Catalog Card Number: 78-66149

Text on pages 34–37, 58–61, 82–85, 104–107,
and all Disney character illustrations
Copyright © 1982, Walt Disney Productions

CONTENTS

1981 AT A GLANCE

JANUARY 1.   Greece became the tenth member of the European Economic Community (EEC). The other members are Belgium, Britain, Denmark, France, Ireland, Italy, Luxembourg, the Netherlands, and West Germany. The EEC, or Common Market, was set up in 1958 to eliminate trade barriers among member nations.

JANUARY 20.   Ronald W. Reagan was sworn in as the 40th president of the United States. George H. Bush was sworn in as the 43rd vice-president.   ■ Iran freed the 52 Americans who had been held hostage for 444 days. They had been captured on November 4, 1979, when Iranians seized the U.S. embassy in Teheran.

MARCH 30.   President Ronald Reagan was shot by a lone gunman outside the Washington Hilton Hotel. The President was rushed to a nearby hospital, where a bullet was removed from his left lung. Also wounded were James Brady, the President's press secretary; Timothy J. McCarthy, a Secret Service agent; and Thomas Delahanty, a District of Columbia policeman. John W. Hinckley, Jr., of Evergreen, Colorado, was arrested at the scene of the attack. He was charged with attempted assassination. (Reagan was hospitalized until April 11.)

APRIL 10.   Based on the 1980 U.S. Census, it was announced that the center of population of the United States is De Soto, Missouri, a small town southwest of St. Louis. The center of population is the point at which the United States would balance if it were a flat surface and every person on it weighed exactly the same. In the country's first census, taken in 1790, the center was just east of Baltimore, Maryland. It has gradually moved westward. Now, for the first time, the center is west of the Mississippi River. It is also farther south than ever before. This reflects the large population growth of the South and Southwest during the 1970's.

APRIL 12. The U.S. space shuttle *Columbia* was launched from Cape Canaveral, Florida. It was the world's first re-usable space craft. With two astronauts aboard, *Columbia* orbited the Earth 36 times. Then, on April 14, it landed in California's Mojave Desert. (A space shuttle is designed to be launched like a rocket and then to return and land like an airplane. It can be used again and again to carry astronauts and instruments into orbit.)

MAY 13. Pope John Paul II, head of the Roman Catholic Church, was shot and seriously wounded. The assassination attempt took place in St. Peter's Square in Rome, Italy, as the Pope stood in an open car moving through a large crowd of worshipers. An escaped Turkish murderer, Mehmet Ali Agca, was arrested for the crime. (The Pope was hospitalized until June 3.)

MAY 21. François Mitterrand, head of the Socialist Party, became president of France. He was France's first leftist president in 23 years.

JUNE 7. Israeli warplanes bombed and destroyed a nuclear reactor near Baghdad, Iraq. Because the reactor was not yet in operation, no radioactivity was released. Israel's prime minister, Menahem Begin, said that the Iraqis had planned to make atomic bombs for use against Israel. The Iraqi Government denied the charge. It said that the reactor was intended for peaceful purposes.

JULY 7. The *Solar Challenger* became the first solar-powered airplane to cross the English Channel. The flight from France to England was 165 miles (266 kilometers) and took nearly 5½ hours. Energy to fly the plane was gathered by 16,000 solar cells on the wings and the tail. These cells changed the sun's energy to electricity, which ran the plane's motor.

AUGUST 19. Two U.S. jet fighters shot down two Libyan jet fighters about 60 miles (100 kilometers) from the coast of Libya. The U.S. Government said that the Libyans had fired first. The incident took place over waters that Libya claims as part of its territory but that the United States says are international waters.

AUGUST 25. The U.S. Voyager 2 space probe flew to within 63,000 miles (101,000 kilometers) of Saturn. It flew much closer to Saturn than did two earlier Voyagers. It also got much closer to some of the planet's 17 known moons. Voyager 2 detected a doughnut-shaped cloud of electrified gases orbiting Saturn. The cloud is the hottest spot ever found in the solar system. It is 300 times hotter than the outer reaches of the sun. Instruments aboard Voyager 2 also detected electrical discharges at least 10,000 times stronger than Earth's lightning.

SEPTEMBER 21. Belize, formerly known as British Honduras, became an independent nation. The Central American country had been ruled by Britain for more than 300 years.

SEPTEMBER 25. Judge Sandra Day O'Connor of Arizona was sworn in as the 102nd justice of the U.S. Supreme Court. She thus became the first woman ever to serve on the Supreme Court.

SEPTEMBER 27. The world's fastest trains began commuter operations between Paris and Lyons, France. The sleek, electrically powered trains have two locomotives, one at each end, and eight passenger cars. The trains ride on special tracks. They cruise at up to 160 miles (257 kilometers) per hour but can go much faster— more than 225 miles (362 kilometers) per hour.

OCTOBER 6. Anwar el-Sadat, president of Egypt, was assassinated as he watched a military parade in Cairo. The attackers were said to be Muslim fanatics. Sadat had been president of Egypt since 1970 and was best known for establishing peace between Egypt and Israel. (In an October 13 referendum, Vice-President Hosni Mubarak was elected to succeed Sadat.)

OCTOBER 18. Prime Minister Wojciech Jaruzelski became head of Poland's Communist Party. He replaced Stanislaw Kania, who was forced to resign by the party's Central Committee. The committee wanted a tougher stand against Solidarity, the independent labor union federation formed in 1980. It also wanted effective action against the country's worsening economic crisis. Food, gasoline, and other essentials had become scarce. And Solidarity had staged a number of strikes and demonstrations demanding more political freedom.

OCTOBER 21. Andreas Papandreou, head of the Panhellenic Socialist Movement, became premier of Greece. He was Greece's first leftist leader in 35 years.

OCTOBER 25. Alberto Salazar, 23, of Massachusetts, won the New York Marathon for the second year in a row. In the process, he ran the fastest marathon ever run, anywhere, anytime: 2 hours, 8 minutes, 13 seconds. The women's winner was Allison Roe, 24, of New Zealand. She also set a world record: 2:25:29. Earlier in the year, Roe had won the Boston Marathon.

NOVEMBER 1. Antigua and Barbuda became an independent nation. The islands, which are located in the Caribbean, had been ruled by Britain for nearly 350 years.

NOVEMBER 14. Astronauts Joe H. Engle and Richard H. Truly ended a 54-hour mission aboard the space shuttle *Columbia*. Although this second mission was shortened because of technical problems, the astronauts completed their major objectives.

DECEMBER 13. Martial law was declared in Poland. The government suspended the operations of Solidarity, the independent labor union federation. It arrested or took into custody many union members, including Solidarity leader Lech Walesa. It also arrested some former government leaders, blaming them for the country's economic crisis. All strikes, demonstrations, and public gatherings were banned. Curfews were imposed, and travel was limited. Soldiers and police patrolled highways and city streets and were stationed in factories and other buildings. And a military council was set up to rule the country. The declaration of martial law canceled the gains in personal freedom that had been won by Solidarity since 1980, when it was founded as the first independent labor union in a Communist country. The government's action had followed a call by Solidarity leaders for a referendum on two questions—confidence in Poland's leaders and the establishment of a non-Communist government. (In the days following the declaration, there were reports of resistance to the government's action. A number of protesters were said to have been killed. While the Soviet Union clearly supported the government, there was no evidence that Soviet troops had been sent to help. On December 20, the Polish ambassador to Washington, Romuald Spasowski, defected to the United States. He said that with martial law, a "cruel night of darkness and silence" had spread over Poland.)

Incredible Creatures

Once upon a time, people believed that the earth was populated by incredible creatures. Some of them were fascinating, but many others were truly horrible beasts.

These animals have never been seen in zoos. And no one has ever taken pictures of them. These creatures never really existed at all—they lived only in people's imaginations. But to the people who believed in them at the time, they were very much alive. They were as real as cats and dogs are to you and me.

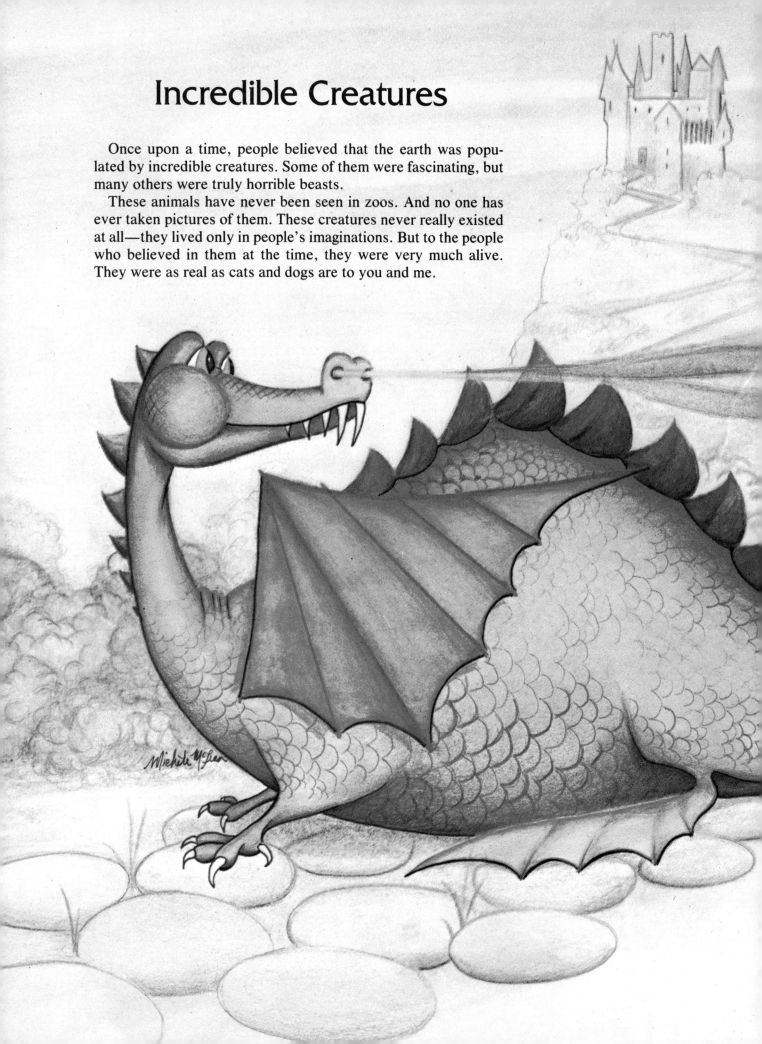

DRAGONS

Dragons are probably the best-known imaginary creatures. Stories about dragons are found in many parts of the world.

A typical dragon had a scaly, snakelike body and four legs with huge claws. The head and front legs were like those of a crocodile, a lion, or an eagle. And many dragons had wings.

In China, Dragon Kings ruled the lakes, rivers, and seas. If people treated them well, the Dragon Kings would see to it that rain watered the farmlands. But if the Dragon Kings believed that they were being treated badly, they would cause droughts or fierce storms.

One Chinese dragon, Ch'ien T'ang, had a terrible temper. When he was angry, he would swing his enormous tail through the sea. This would cause a huge wave of water to sweep over the land. The water would drown villages and cause many deaths.

Chinese dragons were said to change themselves into other living things. Sometimes there were ways to see through their disguises. People thought that a dragon disguised as a fish would speak in a human voice while it was being cooked. But it would be more difficult to detect a dragon that had turned itself into a beautiful young woman.

In Europe during the Dark Ages, dragons were thought to be evil animals. They breathed fire and puffed smoke through their nostrils. Often, groups of three or four would entwine their tails and fly together through the air in search of food. Dragons ate cows, sheep, and people. And they had huge appetites. It was said that one dragon, kept as a pet by a man in Rome, had eaten 6,000 people a day.

MANTICORES

Manticores were fearsome creatures that were said to have originated in India. A manticore had a human face, with blue or gray eyes and a bright red complexion. Reaching from ear to ear was a wide mouth containing three rows of teeth.

A manticore had the body of a lion and a

scorpionlike tail. The tail was covered with poisonous spines. If angry or frightened, a manticore would shoot these spines at its enemies.

Manticores could run very fast. They were powerful, fearsome creatures that could easily catch, knock down, and kill people.

BASILISKS

Basilisks were small poisonous reptiles, each one having a crownlike crest on top of its head. They were thought to be so poisonous that just looking at or smelling one was enough to kill a person or animal.

It was said that if a hunter speared a basilisk, the creature's poison would rise up through the spear and instantly kill him.

CENTICHORAS

The centichora was another mythical native of India. The body of a centichora was part lion and part horse. It ended in an elephantlike tail. The monster had a large round snout, eyes that were very close together, and a human voice. On top of its head were two very long, sharp horns. A centichora could move its horns, which was a great advantage during a fight.

A centichora's worst enemy was the basilisk. The venomous basilisk would bite the centichora while it was sleeping. The basilisk's poison would cause the centichora to swell up like a balloon and die.

THE CHIMERA

The Chimera was another fire-breathing creature. It was found in the mythology of the ancient Greeks. Homer, the famous poet of ancient Greece, described the Chimera as having the head of a lion, the body of a goat, and the tail of a serpent.

One story says that the Chimera was born from a mountain. The mountain had a volcano at the top, goat pastures on its side, and a colony of snakes living at its base.

The fire-breathing Chimera would creep into villages at night and kill all the inhabitants. Finally, a young Greek named Bellerophon set out to destroy the terrible beast. Bellerophon was helped by a powerful winged horse, Pegasus, that could soar like a bird through the sky. Astride Pegasus, Bellerophon flew high above the hiding place of the Chimera and slew it with arrows.

UNICORNS

Most people agreed that unicorns were beautiful animals. A unicorn was built like a horse, with a white body, purple head, and blue eyes. In the center of its forehead was a long, powerful horn. Some writers said the horn was twisted. Others said it was smooth.

One description said that the horn was white at the base, black in the middle, and red at the tip.

People believed that the powder made by crushing a unicorn horn would improve their health. During the 16th and 17th centuries, unicorn powder was sold in most European pharmacies. The powder was used as a cure for epilepsy and as an antidote to poison.

Kings, queens, and other royalty, who often worried that their enemies might try to poison them, used whole unicorn horns as drinking cups. They believed that the magical power of the horn protected them against being poisoned. Unicorn horns were thus very valuable and could only be bought for huge sums of money.

Where did people get the horns of this imaginary animal? Some horns were probably rhinoceros horns. Twisted horns probably came from the narwhal, a type of whale that has a long tusk. And unicorn powder could have been made by crushing the bones of any animal.

Unicorns were said to run so fast that they were very difficult to catch. There are many medieval tapestries and other works of art that show the hunt for the unicorn.

Unicorns were usually described as fierce animals. Yet a unicorn would be very gentle with a maiden. It would allow itself to be petted and even lie down and put its head on a maiden's lap. As a result, the unicorn became a symbol of purity. This is why it is often included in religious paintings.

The Chinese also had a unicorn. It was called Chin-Lin and was different from the European unicorn. Chin-Lin had the body of a deer, the feet of a horse, and the tail of an ox. Its horn was short and made of flesh.

Chin-Lin was a very gentle animal. It always walked carefully in order not to trample small animals on the ground.

CENTAURS

A centaur was half man and half horse. It had the head, arms, and chest of a man. The rest of its body was like the body of a horse.

Centaurs were said to have lived in ancient Greece. Most of them were nasty creatures who broke laws and fought with the Greeks. But one of them, Chiron, was famous for his goodness and intelligence. Chiron taught some of the most important heroes of ancient Greece, including Hercules and Achilles.

Unlike the other centaurs, Chiron was immortal—he could live forever. But in a battle between Hercules and the centaurs, Chiron was accidentally wounded. The wound didn't heal, and it caused Chiron great pain. The supreme god, Zeus, finally allowed Chiron to die. But Chiron is still with us. Zeus placed him among the stars as the constellation Sagittarius.

GUYASCUTUS

This critter was an American invention. It was first described in 1846 as "a monster of gigantic proportions." Specific details of the guyascutus varied greatly. Some people said it was the size of a deer, with rabbit ears and teeth like a mountain lion's. But everyone agreed on one thing: The legs of the animal were longer on one side than on the other. This made it easy for the animal to climb mountains and graze on steep hillsides.

A group of men said they had captured the guyascutus—or gyanousa, as it was sometimes called. The men traveled around the countryside to show it in a tent. At each place they stopped, a crowd of curious people would pay to see the animal. But as soon

as the audience had gathered in the tent, the men would rush in and shout, "The gyanousa am loose!" The terrified customers would run for their lives—leaving behind all the money they had paid and, of course, never seeing the fabulous beast.

GRIFFINS

A griffin had a lion's body and the head and wings of an eagle. Most griffins had four lionlike legs. Others had front legs like an eagle's and hind legs like a lion's.

The griffins of the Middle Ages had an appetite for people. If a griffin caught someone, people thought, it could quickly tear the victim apart with its claws. A griffin's claws were so large and powerful that the creature could fly through the air carrying a horse or even an elephant.

The griffin was a popular symbol of strength. Many European noble families included griffins in their coats of arms.

If you've read Lewis Carroll's *Alice's Adventures in Wonderland,* you've met a griffin. This was the creature that took Alice to meet the Mock Turtle. Alice "did not quite like the look" of the griffin. But they got along well together—much better than did the people and griffins of the Middle Ages.

There were many other strange and fabulous creatures that once existed on earth—yet never really existed at all. Have you ever read about any? Have you ever imagined one of your own?

SLEEP IN AN ELEPHANT

Let's sleep in an enormous elephant . . . or in a cement tepee. Let's snap a photo of the Santa Maria House, a copy of one of Christopher Columbus' ships with a mast going right through the ceiling. And let's take a gander at the marvelous Mother Goose House.

These are just some of the many unusual buildings that people have created. They are used as homes, hotels, motels, or restaurants. They can be found everywhere—from big cities to small towns. There's a teapot-shaped building, complete with handle and spout, in Washington. There's the Pig House in Texas. And in Pennsylvania, there's the Shoe House. Next to it is a smaller shoe house for the family dog. Even the mailbox is in the shape of a shoe. Who built this wonder? Why, a shoemaker, of course.

21

Music boxes, like this newly made carousel and antique birdcage, are enjoyed by people everywhere.

THE MECHANICAL MUSIC MAKER

Once upon a time a portable radio who was strolling along a seaside beach struck up a conversation with a little music box. "I hope you won't be offended if I ask you a personal question," said the radio, "but how do you music boxes manage to survive in today's electronic world? Shouldn't you be extinct by now?"

Thorens Treasury of Music Boxes

At one point in history, for a period of about 100 years, the music box reigned supreme as a source of automatically made music. Music boxes could be found in taverns, ice cream parlors, and in almost every home. And they played all kinds of songs, even the melodies of famous composers such as Beethoven, Haydn, and Mozart. Today, in our electronic world of radios and stereos, the gentle music box has survived very well, and it is still enjoyed by people everywhere.

LITTLE BOXES OF SOUND

A music box is a mechanical, self-playing instrument that plays tunes when it is wound up like a clock. The sounds it produces are usually soft, delicate, and high pitched.

The first music boxes were made by Swiss watchmakers in the late 1700's. They were tiny mechanisms that were encased in luxury items such as watches, snuff boxes, perfume bottles, and walking sticks. They played only simple tunes, and often the mechanism created such a loud noise that the little melody was drowned out. In these early music boxes, the music was secondary to the use of the item.

As the mechanisms were improved, music boxes began to be made as entertainment items in their own right. By the early 1800's, music boxes that were operated by a cylinder mechanism had become popular musical instruments. At first they were made for

their musical qualities rather than for appearance, and they were enclosed in simple wood boxes.

In the mid-1800's, the art of the cabinet-maker joined that of the music box maker, and elaborate cases were designed. Mother-of-pearl, colored wood, and precious metals were used as inlay on the tops and fronts of the boxes. They were often worked into designs with musical motifs, such as mandolins and harps. Birds and flowers were also popular designs. Larger music boxes were often custom-made in the form of writing desks, ladies' cabinets, and other pieces of furniture for the home.

Around 1850, little drums and bells were added to the mechanisms of some music boxes. These were the forerunners of the spectacular orchestra boxes. Orchestra boxes included a set of bells, a snare drum, a wood drum that produced the sound of castanets, and sometimes a triangle or a gong.

Automata were elaborate music boxes that were very popular during Victorian times. These music boxes had figures of people and animals that played little instruments, danced, and clacked castanets while the music played. Magicians, monkeys, and acrobats performed tricks. Miniature birds in cages flapped their wings and whistled songs. Horses and riders galloped as miniature carousels spun around. The music did

This bell-and-drum box shows "castanets" on the left, bells in the center, and a drum on the right.

not come from the figures but from a tiny cylinder mechanism in the base of the box.

Despite continuing improvements, most cylinder music boxes could play only a few melodies. And interchangeable cylinders were very expensive. In the late 1800's, the cylinder music box was replaced by the disc music box. The discs were a standard size and interchangeable—they could be changed like records. They were immensely popular. At the beginning of the 20th century, an automatic disc-changing device was introduced.

Thomas Edison invented the phonograph in 1877. But it was more than 25 years before this instrument, with its scratchy, squeaky music, was so improved that it overtook the

Automata music boxes had figures of people or animals that played little musical instruments while the music played. The music came from a tiny cylinder mechanism in the base of the music box.

In the late 1800's, the cylinder music box was replaced by the disc music box. The discs could be changed like records. (The bar across the disc is holding the disc in place.)

LOOK INSIDE A MUSIC BOX

If you open a music box and look inside, you will probably see a cylinder mechanism. The cylinder has small metal pins sticking out of it. The pins may look as if they are helter-skelter, but they have been arranged in a certain order to produce a melody. Parallel to the cylinder is what looks like a steel comb. The teeth of the comb are of varying lengths, and they are tuned to the musical scale.

Now, when you turn the key of the music box, you wind up a spring. The spring sets gears in motion, and the gears turn the cylinder. As the cylinder rotates, the pins pluck the teeth of the comb. The teeth vibrate and produce delicate, tinkly sounds. The longer teeth on the comb produce the lower notes of the melody, and the shorter teeth produce the higher notes.

Cylinders in old music boxes were usually programmed to play several tunes. And some boxes contained more than one cylinder.

A disc music box contains a metal disc instead of a cylinder, and a steel comb. The disc, which looks like a record, has punched-out projections on the underside. The projections are arranged to produce a melody. As the disc rotates, the projections cause small star-shaped wheels to turn, which pluck the tuned teeth of the comb.

Large disc music boxes, with interchangeable discs, were very popular in the late 1800's and early 1900's.

music box in popularity. Gradually, music boxes disappeared from taverns, ice cream parlors, and living rooms. They went into attics, cellars, and barns.

Over the years, collectors have been digging out old music boxes from their hiding places and restoring them. Why don't you go on a treasure hunt? If you're lucky, you just may find an antique music box that your parents or grandparents stored away. If you find one, wind it up and listen to the sweet, tinkling tune. You may hear anything from *The William Tell Overture* to "Gently Over the Pimples, John," a favorite played in barber shops when men were getting a shave.

Perhaps you would like to start a collection of music boxes—both old and new ones. Although the elaborate orchestra boxes are of a past era, it's easy to find fascinating new music boxes in the form of jewelry cases, toys, birds, and Swiss chalets. It's even possible to buy a do-it-yourself music box kit. This includes a musical movement, with tunes of your choice, and rotating or stationary bases for mounting figurines and craftwork. By creating your own music box, you may enjoy all the more the gentle tunes from the little boxes of sound.

HARRY GOLDSMITH
Former patent counsel

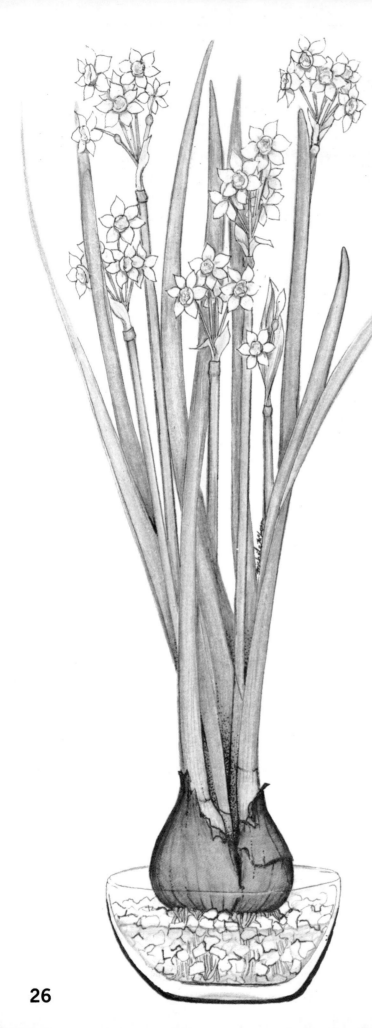

HOW TO FOOL FLOWERS

In cold climates, winter can be a dull time of year. The bright leaves and colorful flowers that adorn the other seasons are missing. But it's very easy to bring this color into your home in winter. You do it by fooling the flowers. You make plants think it's spring by bringing them into the warmth of the house. The plants respond by blooming early. This process is called forcing.

Hyacinths, tulips, crocuses, and other bulb plants can be forced, either in water or soil. First, the bulbs must be stored in a cold place for two to three months. During this time they grow a root system, and tips of green leaves begin to poke up at the top. Then, when the bulbs are given warmth and light, the leaves and stem shoot up. Soon the plant blossoms. Some bulbs, such as the paper-white narcissus, have been especially developed for indoor forcing—they are ready to grow even without the cold period.

Budded branches from trees that flower in the spring can also be forced. Forsythia, pussy willow, flowering quince, cherry, and apple blossoms are especially easy to force. The closer to spring you cut the branches, the quicker they will blossom.

Here are directions for forcing three kinds of flowers. Try these—and then experiment with others.

PAPER-WHITE NARCISSUS

Fill a shallow bowl with about a cup of clean pebbles. Place one or more bulbs on the pebbles so that the pointed ends are up. Spread more pebbles around the bulbs, and then arrange the bulbs so that they will stand up straight. Add water to the bowl. The water should barely touch the bottoms of the bulbs. Add water as necessary to keep it at this level.

Put the bowl in a cool, light place such as a windowsill. When the leaves are several inches high, move the bowl to a warmer spot. (Avoid putting the bulbs in a very warm room or near a radiator. The heat may cause the flower buds to dry up.) A few weeks later, clusters of fragrant white flowers will burst forth. (Paper-whites also come in yellow, but they take longer to force.)

HYACINTHS

Choose a vase or jar with a narrow opening. You want the bulb to sit on the opening. Fill the vase with room-temperature water. Set the bulb, pointed side up, so that its bottom barely touches the water.

Put the vase in a cold, dark place, but one where the temperature won't fall below freezing. When a good root system has developed—about eight weeks—bring the vase into a cool place in the house. A few days later, move the vase into a warm, light room and wait for the flowers to blossom.

FORSYTHIA

By early February you can cut branches from a forsythia bush and bring them indoors. Cutting should be done on a day when the temperature is above freezing. Choose branches with plump, well-developed buds. Cut off the branches with a sharp pair of clippers. Never try to pull or break off branches. This can hurt the bush. Arrange the branches in a vase filled with room-temperature water. Change the water every few days. Put the branches where they will get a lot of light. In a few weeks, the branches will be wreathed with bright yellow flowers.

27

THE SPACE SHUTTLE COLUMBIA

FUEL TANK

BOOSTER ROCKETS

ORBITER

The space shuttle *Columbia* was launched for the first time on April 12, 1981.

On April 12, 1981, the United States launched the first space shuttle—a vehicle unlike any ever sent aloft. The shuttle *Columbia* did something no spacecraft had ever done. It returned safely to Earth, ready to be refitted and flown again.

Before *Columbia,* all spacecraft were boosted into orbit by powerful, expensive rocket assemblies. Each spacecraft and rocket assembly was used only once. Scientists at the National Aeronautics and Space Administration (NASA) reasoned that vehicles that could be used for more than one flight might save millions of dollars in future space ventures.

The result was the space shuttle, which is launched like a rocket, orbits like a spacecraft, and glides to a landing like an airplane.

THE FIRST LAUNCH

April 12 was a clear, sunny day in Cape Canaveral, Florida. At the Kennedy Space Center, the shuttle stood ready on its launching pad, its four parts visible to observers half a mile away. Looming tallest was the huge external fuel tank, filled with liquid hydrogen and liquid oxygen. It was flanked by two 15-story-high solid-fuel booster rockets. And astride the tank was the shuttle orbiter *Columbia,* a delta-winged craft about the size of a DC-9 jet.

The cabin at the front of the orbiter had been designed to hold up to seven people. But for the first flight, only two were aboard. In command of *Columbia* was John W. Young. He had made four previous space flights, including two trips to the moon. With him was Robert L. Crippen, who had been an astronaut for years but had never been in space.

At 7:00 A.M., right on schedule, *Columbia*'s three internal, liquid-fueled engines fired. They were followed two seconds later by the external booster rockets. The shuttle slowly lifted off the ground on a column of smoke and fire. The heat and blast from the engines were so great that parts of the launch pad were badly damaged.

The shuttle streaked skyward, gaining speed and rolling over so that the orbiter rode belly-up under the fuel tank. Two minutes after launch, *Columbia* reached an altitude of about 28 miles (45 kilometers), and both booster rockets were detached. Parachutes lowered them gently into the Atlantic Ocean, where recovery ships waited. The rockets were towed to shore to be used again.

Eight minutes after launch, *Columbia* had reached a speed of 16,800 miles (27,000 kilometers) an hour. It had drained the external fuel tank. The main engines were shut down, and the tank was released. (Most of the tank—the only part of the shuttle designed not to be used again—burned up in the atmosphere.) Then *Columbia*'s smaller maneuvering engines guided the craft into orbit— nearly 170 miles (275 kilometers) above Earth.

ON BOARD COLUMBIA

Once in orbit, Young and Crippen could move weightlessly about the pressurized, air-filled front cabin. *Columbia* had been designed so that scientists and others could travel into space with a minimum of training. The facilities aboard were far more comfortable than those on the earlier Apollo and Gemini craft. *Columbia* was equipped with an oven, hot and cold water, a zero-gravity toilet, and special sleeping compartments. On this trip, however, bulky flight instruments were stored in the sleeping area. The two astronauts had to sleep in their seats.

The main purpose of *Columbia*'s first flight was to make sure the craft could go up and come back safely. One of the most important steps in the mission was to test the doors to the huge cargo bay. It was feared that heat from the sun or stress during lift-off might distort the doors, so that they would jam open or shut. Fortunately, the doors worked perfectly.

One problem involved the heat-resistant tiles that covered the orbiter. The tiles were intended to protect *Columbia* from the intense heat caused by friction with the atmosphere when the craft returned to Earth. Designing and attaching the tiles had proved quite a problem when *Columbia* was built. Now, with the craft safely in orbit, a televi-

Astronauts John Young and Robert Crippen, shown during a preflight test, flew *Columbia* on its first mission.

sion camera mounted in the tail showed that some tiles were missing. It was feared that if too many tiles had been loosened by launch vibrations, the orbiter could become dangerously hot on re-entry. But luckily, only a few tiles had been lost, and the heat-resistant pads beneath them were intact.

In all, *Columbia* circled the Earth 36 times, each orbit taking about 90 minutes. At about noon on April 14, Young and Crippen began the trip home.

With the craft traveling tail first over the Indian Ocean, the maneuvering engines fired again. This burst of power slowed the shuttle, and it began to descend. When *Columbia* re-entered the atmosphere, friction turned its skin a glowing red with heat.

As *Columbia* approached the coast of California, Young took over the controls from the computer that had been guiding the craft. This was a critical part of the flight. Unlike an airplane, the shuttle cannot circle the landing strip and try again if the pilot makes a bad approach. Young sent the craft into a series of curves that further slowed it. Then, at 1:21 P.M., he brought *Columbia* to a perfect landing on a dry lake bed at Edwards Air Force Base in California. The shuttle touched down at twice the speed of a landing jet airliner.

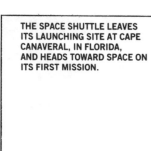

THE SPACE SHUTTLE LEAVES ITS LAUNCHING SITE AT CAPE CANAVERAL, IN FLORIDA, AND HEADS TOWARD SPACE ON ITS FIRST MISSION.

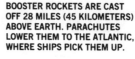

BOOSTER ROCKETS ARE CAST OFF 28 MILES (45 KILOMETERS) ABOVE EARTH. PARACHUTES LOWER THEM TO THE ATLANTIC, WHERE SHIPS PICK THEM UP.

WHEN THE SHUTTLE'S EXTERNAL FUEL TANK IS EMPTY, THE MAIN ENGINES SHUT DOWN AND THE TANK IS DETACHED.

THE SHUTTLE'S MANEUVERING ENGINES BEGIN TO NUDGE THE CRAFT INTO AN ORBIT NEARLY 170 MILES (275 KILOMETERS) ABOVE THE EARTH. THIS FINAL ORBIT IS REACHED ABOUT 7 HOURS INTO THE FLIGHT.

THE SECOND FLIGHT

After a thorough inspection, *Columbia* was carried piggy-back on a 747 aircraft to Cape Canaveral. There it was made ready for its second flight, on November 12, 1981. This mission was much like the first. But astronauts Joe H. Engle and Richard H. Truly were asked to perform more experiments.

Columbia's cargo bay carried equipment

In the future, the shuttle might be used to construct a craft that would ferry people and materials to the moon.

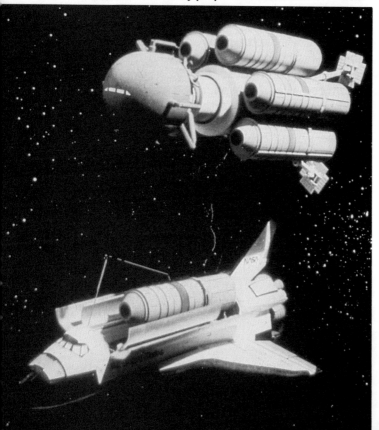

to map geological features with radar. The ship also scanned the Earth with an infrared device that can detect mineral deposits, and it observed the distribution of plant life in the oceans. Testing *Columbia*'s manipulator arm was another important part of the second flight. This remote-control mechanical arm can pluck items from the cargo bay and place satellites in orbit.

The second mission was supposed to last five days. But it was cut short when one of the craft's three fuel cells, which provide electrical power, failed. *Columbia* touched down at Edwards on November 14, after 54 hours and 36 revolutions of the Earth.

FUTURE USES OF THE SHUTTLE

With a cargo bay the size of a railroad boxcar, the shuttle has been called a "space truck." Its main job will be to carry people and equipment into space and bring them safely back to Earth. Here are some of the uses scientists foresee for the shuttle:

• Communications and military satellites can be carried up in the cargo bay and placed in orbit by the manipulator arm. Technicians on the shuttle can service satellites in space, or the satellites can be brought back to Earth for repair. The shuttle could also carry up pieces of large satellites—huge antennas or solar power stations, perhaps—to be assembled in space.

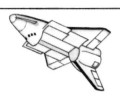

IN ORBIT, THE ASTRONAUTS TEST THE CARGO BAY DOORS, FLIGHT CONTROL SYSTEMS, AND DATA PROCESSING SYSTEMS. THEY ALSO CONDUCT MANEUVERING TESTS. FLIGHT PROGRESS REPORTS ARE TELEVISED, AND THE ASTRONAUTS HAVE TWO SLEEP PERIODS.

THE CARGO BAY DOORS ARE CLOSED. WITH THE SHUTTLE TRAVELING TAIL FIRST, THE MANEUVERING ENGINES ARE FIRED TO SLOW THE CRAFT, AND IT BEGINS TO DESCEND.

ABOUT HALF AN HOUR LATER, THE SHUTTLE RE-ENTERS THE EARTH'S ATMOSPHERE. ITS SKIN GLOWS RED-HOT FROM THE FRICTION OF RE-ENTRY.

THE SHUTTLE MAKES A PERFECT LANDING ON A DRY LAKE BED AT EDWARDS AIR FORCE BASE IN THE CALIFORNIA DESERT. GROUND CREWS CHECK THE CRAFT BEFORE THE ASTRONAUTS LEAVE IT.

• Deep-space probes can be carried into a low orbit by the shuttle. From there, the probes can fire their rockets to begin the trip to the edge of the solar system.

• Space is an ideal place to study many things—the sun, solar wind, comets, radiation, and the effects of weightlessness, to name just a few. So an orbiting laboratory, Spacelab, has been designed to fit neatly in the shuttle's cargo bay. The first Spacelab is being built by the European Space Agency. It will be made up of pressurized compartments (where scientists can work in their shirtsleeves) and instrument-carrying pallets that will be exposed to space. Spacelab will ride up and back with the shuttle, but future laboratories may be designed to stay in space.

• The shuttle is also scheduled to carry a 12-ton space telescope into orbit. Because it will be beyond the Earth's atmosphere, this telescope will be able to see much farther into space than telescopes on Earth. It will use solar energy to beam information back to Earth.

• Shuttle flights will test the possibility of manufacturing in space. The weightless and near-vacuum conditions of space seem to be ideal for making certain products. Among them are very pure silicon crystals, glass products for use in lasers and fiber optics, and certain biological materials.

Columbia is designed to fly about 100 missions, each a week to a month long. There is still uncertainty over how reliable, costly, and useful the shuttle will be. But by 1985, NASA hopes to have three more orbiters—*Challenger, Discovery,* and *Atlantis.*

BENEDICT A. LEERBURGER
Editor in Chief
Gateways to Science (3rd edition)

One day, the shuttle may even build space stations, putting the parts in place with its manipulator arm.

Young artists can develop their talents at a special museum in the Soviet Union.

Circus, by a 13-year-old artist, is formed of colorful scraps of fabric.

Improvisation, by a 7-year-old Soviet artist, was created from colorful yarns.

YOUNG ARTISTS

The pictures on these pages are on display in a special museum—one of the few museums in the world devoted completely to children's art. The museum is in the city of Yerevan, in the Armenian Soviet Socialist Republic in the Soviet Union. It was founded over ten years ago, and it has a collection of more than 100,000 works of art. The museum also has a studio, where young people can use new art materials and learn new techniques. Thus the museum is really an art center, with two goals. One is to help young artists develop their talents. The other is to study children's art as a separate branch of art—art that is expressive and closely linked to fantasy.

BIRD-BRAINED BIRDWATCHERS

Professor Nefarious sat glumly at his desk in the College of Criminal Knowledge. "Hey, Professor," said Sidney, inspecting his fingernails. "When are we gonna pull another job?"

"Yeah, Boss. We been sittin' around for weeks," complained Armadillo. "We ain't learnin' no criminal knowledge."

"Alas, my boys," replied Professor Nefarious, "I simply can't get excited about crime lately." He got up and began to pace the floor. "Here I am, Professor Nefarious, the world authority on criminal knowledge, and no one even knows my name. Boys," he sighed, "fame has passed me by.

"And worst of all," Nefarious added, "that incompetent Sleuth makes headlines every other day!"

"But, Boss, the *Times* doesn't print the names of criminals unless they're serving time," Armadillo pointed out.

Fliplip looked up from the comic section he was reading. "You could get arrested, Boss. Then you'd get your name in the paper."

"Idiot!" snapped the Professor, and he grabbed the newspaper from Fliplip and smacked him on the head. "I might have known I couldn't depend on . . .

"Wait a minute!" The professor returned to his desk and spread the newspaper out in front of him. It carried Sleuth's picture on the front page, along with a story about the upcoming Record Birdwatch, in which Sleuth, "London's Greatest Detective and Noted Birdwatcher," was scheduled to take part.

"I have it!" crowed Nefarious. "I'll get my name in the paper and beat that nincompoop Sleuth, all at the same time. Boys, your beloved Professor is going to be the next Record Birdwatcher!"

"But, Professor—you don't know anything about watching birds," said Sidney.

"Fool," answered the Professor. "I can learn enough to act like a birdwatcher. Besides, you don't think I'm going to do this legit, do you? Now, listen . . ."

The following morning, as Sleuth was getting his gear ready for the Record Birdwatch, Mickey was reading the morning *Times*. "I say, Sleuth, here's something odd," he called. "It seems the Natural History Museum was robbed last night and . . ."

"Oh, confound it," interrupted Sleuth, "where have I put my field glasses? Mickey, have you seen them?"

"They're hanging on the strap around your neck, Sleuth," replied Mickey. "Now, pay attention. Someone has stolen the museum's collection of stuffed birds and an-

tique birdcalls. You must offer our help to track down the thieves."

"Oh, I will, Mickey, just as soon as today's Record Birdwatch is over. But right now, I must concentrate on holding on to my position as Best Birdwatcher of Britain. If I sight 73 different birds today, I'll break my own record."

"That's all very well, Sleuth," grumbled his friend, "but it seems to me that our first duty is to fight crime."

"Pish-tush, Mickey," answered Sleuth. "Today our first duty is to watch birds."

At nine o'clock sharp that morning, the birders assembled at the Hyde Park Bird Preserve. Mickey and Sleuth were shocked to find Professor Nefarious one of their group. When Sleuth questioned him, Nefarious explained that he had decided to go straight.

"Yes, Sleuth, I have seen the light," he said. "No longer will we be enemies. Now we will be fellow birdwatchers on the sky-way of life."

Sleuth was delighted to believe Nefarious. "Isn't it just wonderful, Mickey?" he burbled. "It must be my own sterling example that has turned that arch-criminal from the error of his ways. It's yet another feather in my cap!"

Mickey wasn't so sure, but he didn't say anything.

"Gentlemen! Gentlemen!" called the referee. "Let us come to order. I shall review the rules of the Record Birdwatch. Last year at this event, 72 different birds were identified by that distinguished birder, Sleuth." He was interrupted by polite applause, and Sleuth took a bow.

The referee continued. "This year, the first birder to sight 73 different birds in a twelve-hour period will have the honor of breaking that record. And I remind you, gentlemen, a bird may be identified by either sight or sound. The first one to see or hear a particular bird gets credit for the sighting, which must be confirmed by me.

"Field glasses at the ready . . ." called the referee. "BEGIN!"

All day long the air was filled with shouts of "There it is! A purple-pinioned-sapsucker!" and "By George, I think I hear a rufous redstart!" and "Eureka! A pileated plover!" By afternoon, Sleuth and Nefarious had each sighted 72 birds, and the tension was building. Suddenly there came a faint *tweet-tweet-wheeooo!*

"Aha! A right tern!" cried Professor Nefarious. "I've done it! I've broken Sleuth's record!" And he turned to the photographers from the *Times* who had accompanied the birdwatching party. "Here, you fellows! Take my picture. It must appear on the front page of the *Times!*"

As flash powder flashed and Nefarious posed, Sleuth did his best to be a good loser.

"He won fair and square," said London's Greatest Detective. "I'm only happy that it was my example that set him on the road to an honest career."

"SLEUTH!" shouted Mickey. "Listen to me!"

When he finally got Sleuth's attention, Mickey dropped a bombshell. "Sleuth," he explained patiently, "the right tern has been extinct for a hundred years. Something funny is going on here."

Sleuth's eyes got round. "You know, Mickey," he said slowly, "the right tern *has*

been extinct for a hundred years. Something funny *is* going on here.''

''I thought you'd never figure it out,'' answered Mickey. ''Now you stay here and keep Nefarious busy. His henchmen are never far away, and if I find them, we'll get to the bottom of this.''

''Listen, Mickey,'' replied Sleuth, ''I'll stay here and keep Nefarious busy. His henchmen can't be far away, and when you find them, we'll get to the bottom of this.''

As Sleuth stepped up to Nefarious and suggested a photo of himself shaking hands with the Professor, Mickey quietly slipped away. As Mickey crept through the bushes, he saw Sidney, Armadillo, and Fliplip. Sidney was holding up a stuffed bird on a stick, while Armadillo got the next one ready. Fliplip stood by, a batch of birdcalls hanging on a string around his neck.

''Well, well, well,'' said Mickey to himself, ''here's a birdwatcher's dream—a trio of fine-feathered jailbirds!'' And he flushed the three students of criminal knowledge right into the arms of Sleuth and his fellow birders.

The game was up. Nefarious was disappointed that his scheme had been uncovered, but he managed to slip away in the confusion. He didn't notice one of the *Times* photographers taking a picture of his retreating back.

The following morning, Nefarious sat all alone in the College of Criminal Knowledge, glumly flipping through the *Times*. He had ripped the front page into little pieces, trying to wipe out the sight of yet another front-page article about Sleuth. London's Greatest Detective had not only won the Record Birdwatch with a sighting of number 73, a spectacled sparrow, but had also solved the theft of the Natural History Museum's collection of stuffed birds and antique birdcalls.

Suddenly, on page 33, the Professor came upon a picture of the back of a figure that looked somehow familiar. Then he recognized it, and he gnashed his teeth in rage as he read the caption: ''Unidentified accomplice of the three famous criminals, Messrs. Sidney, Armadillo, and Fliplip, who were arrested late yesterday by Sleuth, London's Greatest Detective.''

PRETTY POTS

Your special plants deserve special pots. Even ordinary plants will look brighter and more cheerful if they are placed in pots that have been designed just for them.

To make these decorative pots, you can use almost any kind of watertight container —a regular clay or plastic flowerpot, a coffee can, an old bucket, or the bottom half of a large plastic bleach bottle.

Match or blend the containers with the decor of the room in which they will be placed. Perhaps there is some fabric left over from a tablecloth made for the kitchen table. Use the leftover fabric on pots that will be in the kitchen. Flower pots that will be kept in your bedroom might be covered with cartoon decals or pictures of racing cars.

Before you begin, make sure that the container is clean and dry. And plan your design on a piece of paper first.

CRAZY CALICO

You'll need a plastic container, scraps of calico or other printed fabrics, scissors, and white glue.

Cut a strip of fabric wide enough to cover the top edge of the container. Cut a second strip wide enough to circle the bottom few inches of the container. Glue the strips in place.

Now cut out a number of triangles of different patterns and sizes. If you use pinking shears, the triangles will have notched edges.

Arrange the triangles in an interesting overlapping design. Try not to put two triangles of the same fabric next to each other. When the arrangement pleases you, glue the triangles onto the container.

PAINTED POTS

You'll need tin cans, acrylic spray paint and poster paints, a paint brush, and decals.

Cover the entire outside of each can with spray paint. After the paint has dried, add painted designs or decals—or both.

Unlike clay and plastic containers, coffee cans and other tin cans should not hold plants directly. The cans, which consist mainly of steel, will rust after a while. It's better to use the tin cans as "jackets" for clay or plastic pots. In fact, this is a good way to hide your old chipped or stained pots.

Put a thin layer of pebbles in the bottom of each tin can before inserting a flowerpot. This makes it easier for excess water to drain away from the plant's roots.

Tin containers can also be decorated with holiday designs. A white can with a green and red holly design painted on it would add a charming touch to any room at Christmastime. A green can with bright red heart decals would be attractive for Valentine's Day. It's easy to substitute these containers for the plants' regular containers for a while.

CLAY CACTI

You'll need a clay (terra cotta) pot and felt-tipped markers in several colors.

Ordinary clay flowerpots can be turned into exciting works of art. They can be covered with many different kinds of designs. Perhaps you might create a group of pots that will hold cactus plants. The pots could be decorated with desert scenes and patterns like those on Indian blankets.

Or design a city street scene, a country meadow, or big bold flowers. Geometric patterns look especially good on clay.

Some colors will work better than others on clay. Browns, bright reds, and dark greens are good. Pale pinks and blues tend to look washed out. Test various colors on the underside of the pot before drawing on the designs.

FELT FUN

You'll need a plastic container, printed fabrics, pieces of felt, scissors, and white glue.

Cover the container with the fabric. You can use one kind of fabric or several kinds with different designs. This will form the background for the felt cutouts that you will paste on.

You can make your own designs for the felt cutouts, or you can trace designs from books. Felt cutouts of your home and some trees could be placed on green polka dots. Bright red felt horses could gallop across a field of yellow flowers. A black felt cat or two could sit on an orange-striped background.

Use felt-tipped markers to add details, such as windows and a door on a house. Green sequins could be used for the cat's eyes.

WRAPPED IN YARN

You'll need a plastic container, yarn in several colors, scissors, and glue.

Draw a line from the top of the container to the bottom. As you wrap the yarn around the container, begin and end all pieces along this line. This side of the container should be placed toward the wall so that people won't see the yarn ends. But try to cover each yarn end with the beginning of the next piece of yarn. This will keep the yarn from unraveling and will give a neater look.

Begin at the top of the container and work downward. Put a thin thread of glue on the container, then press and briefly hold the yarn in place. Keep the rows horizontal and evenly spaced.

This bristlecone pine, in California, is the oldest living thing in the world.

THE OLDEST LIVING THING

On a dry, rocky slope in the White Mountains of California, there's a tree that's almost 5,000 years old. It's the oldest living thing in the world.

The tree is a bristlecone pine. It sprouted from a seed about 2800 B.C.—before the great pyramids of Egypt were built. By the time of Moses it was already 1,500 years old. When Jesus was born it was close to 3,000 years old. When Columbus came to America it was more than 4,000 years old.

The tree hasn't had an easy life. It lives high on a mountain where it is exposed to fierce winds and winter storms. Sometimes the temperature falls below freezing. At other times the hot sun bakes the land. There is very little rain.

The tree shows its age and the results of its hard life. Its trunk and branches are bent and twisted. The wind has worn away much of the bark on its trunk and the soil from its roots.

Nevertheless, each year the tree grows a ring of new wood. The rings tell us how old the tree is. Scientists use a tool called a borer to remove a core of wood from the tree. The core is like a long, thin pencil. Scientists look at the core under a microscope so they can see and count the rings. The rings are very, very thin because the tree grows very

slowly. It may take a bristlecone pine 100 years to grow 1 inch (2.5 centimeters) wider, and 20 years to grow 1 inch taller.

There are several other bristlecone pines in the White Mountains that are more than 4,000 years old. And scientists have found very old bristlecone pines in Utah, Colorado, Arizona, and New Mexico. Wind and weather have taken their toll on these trees, too. In many cases, only a small part of the tree is alive—perhaps just a narrow band of wood leading from the soil to a few living branches. But this actually helps the tree survive. Because the living branches are so few, the tree needs very little water.

Bristlecone pine trees are named after their cones, which are dark brown and about 3 inches (7.5 centimeters) long. Each of the cone's thick scales ends in a long bristlelike spine. The trees have short, dark green needles (leaves) that grow in bundles of five. The bark is reddish-brown. The cones, needles, and bark are often covered with a sticky sap, or resin. The resin protects the trees from insect pests and diseases. It helps the trees live for thousands of years.

No one knows how much longer the oldest bristlecone pine will live . . . or which trees of today will still be alive 5,000 years from now.

Alexander the Great, King of Macedonia, was one of the most famous warriors of ancient times. He also helped to spread Greek culture to millions of people under his rule.

This marble head of Alexander was found in Pella, the capital of ancient Macedonia and the birthplace of Alexander.

THE SEARCH FOR ALEXANDER

Alexander the Great was one of the most famous people who ever lived. His fame is well deserved. By the time he was 18 he was commanding troops in battle. At 20 he became king of Macedonia, a country north of the ancient Greek city-states. In the next twelve years he conquered a vast amount of territory. He extended his kingdom as far east as India and as far south as Egypt. But Alexander was more than a great warrior. He introduced new ideas for governing conquered countries. And one of his major contributions to world history was the spread of Greek culture to millions of people living in the countries under his rule.

The culture and civilization of Alexander's time—the 4th century B.C.—was brought alive by a stunning exhibit that toured the United States from late 1980 through early 1982. Called ''The Search for Alexander,'' the exhibit showed the objects that the ancient Greeks had used in their homes, for adornment, and for worship. There were also more recent items that were inspired by the legends of Alexander.

Alexander's Time. Alexander was born in Pella, Macedonia, in 356 B.C., some 2,300 years ago. His father was Philip II, king of Macedonia from 359 to 336 B.C. When Alexander was 13, he

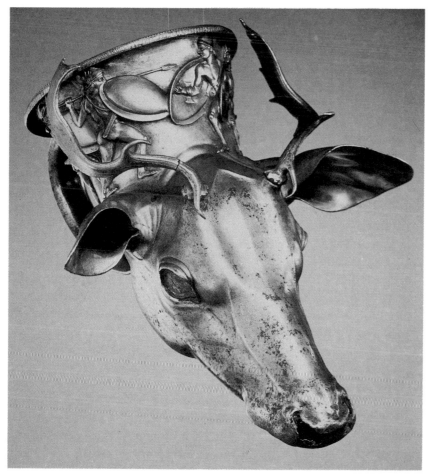

These ancient objects—a silver drinking horn and a silver container decorated with a portrait of Heracles—were included in an exhibit that brought alive the culture and civilization of Alexander's time.

became a pupil of the Greek philosopher Aristotle. From this great teacher, Alexander learned much about Greek culture, and he became deeply attached to it.

Alexander's father was also a great warrior. Philip developed a superb army and used it to make Macedonia the most powerful country in Europe. He conquered most of the city-states of Greece and ruled over much of the land to the north and northwest of Macedonia as well. Philip was assassinated as he prepared to invade Greece's main enemy, Persia.

With Philip's death and Alexander's ascension to the throne, southern Greece tried to break away from Macedonian rule. Alexander led his troops south and crushed the rebellion. He reunited the cities of Greece and became their leader. Then he turned to the countries of Asia and Africa. He conquered Persia and Egypt and began an invasion of India. He never lost a battle. His military successes fulfilled the desires of his father, who had once said, "My son, look for a kingdom worthy of yourself. Macedonia is too small for you."

When Alexander was only 32 years old, he died of a fever. His body was wrapped in gold cloth and placed in a beautiful coffin. He was buried in Alexandria, a city he had founded in Egypt. At the time of his death, he had been the leader of the largest Western empire of the ancient world. And throughout this empire, he

Philip II, Alexander's father, was also a great warrior-king.

43

had spread the Greek way of life—language, customs, art, games, philosophy, and education.

The Exhibit. Many of the ancient treasures in the exhibit had been found in graves. Graves are a major source of archeological material. Objects buried in graves are protected and are less likely to decay or break than objects kept above ground.

The people of ancient Greece believed in an afterlife—a life after death. Thus they buried with a dead person those things that might be needed in the afterlife: weapons, armor, containers for food and drink. These objects tell us a lot about life during Alexander's time.

From the exhibit, we can see that the people of Alexander's time took great pride in the containers created by their artisans. These included huge bowls, storage jars, drinking cups, pitchers, and vases. The containers are made of metal—gold, silver, iron, and bronze. Some of the containers are decorated with designs and portraits, often of mythological beings. Heracles, a mythical hero known for his strength, was a popular subject.

An outstanding example of metalwork is a huge bronze krater, or vase, found in a grave at Derveni in northern Greece. The vase is 3 feet (90 centimeters) tall. It was used for mixing wine and water. Its decorations show the wedding of Dionysus and Ariadne. (In Greek mythology, Dionysus was the god of wine, and Ariadne was the daughter of King Minos of Crete.)

The highlights of the show were magnificent objects found in a tomb in Vergina, a Greek village in what was once ancient Macedonia. The tomb was uncovered in 1977 by Greek archeologist Manolis Andronikos. It was filled with armor and beautiful ceremonial objects made of precious metals.

When Andronikos opened the marble coffin in the main cham-

Also in the exhibit was this huge bronze vase, showing the wedding of Dionysus and Ariadne. It is an outstanding example of the metalwork made by the artisans of Alexander's time.

The highlights of the show were magnificent objects found in a tomb that may be that of Philip II. This solid gold casket is decorated with a sunburst, the symbol of all the Macedonian kings. Inside the casket was a . . .

ber of the tomb, he found a solid gold casket decorated with a sunburst, the symbol of the Macedonian kings. Inside the casket were the remains of a man, covered with a gold wreath of oak leaves and acorns. (The oak tree was the sacred tree of Zeus, the most important god in ancient Greece.) There was also a gilded silver diadem. This adjustable hoop was worn on the head to indicate that the wearer of it was a ruler. Archeologists had known of diadems from portraits of kings on coins. But this was the first time that an actual diadem had been found. Obviously, the tomb was no ordinary tomb. It was the tomb of a very special person.

Andronikos believes that Vergina was once the ancient burial place of the kings of Macedonia. He believes the tomb is that of Philip II, Alexander's father. There is no absolute proof that this is true, but the evidence supports the belief. The richness of the objects in the tomb suggests a royal owner. All the objects date from between 350 and 325 B.C. During this time only one king, Philip II, was buried in Macedonia. The bones in the casket were those of a man of approximately 46, Philip's age at the time of his death. And the greaves, or leg armor, found in the tomb consist of two unequal pieces. The greave for one leg is shorter than the other. Philip, who was lame, probably would have needed unequal greaves.

If it is true that the objects found in Vergina belonged to Philip II, then they are the objects that Alexander actually lived with too. But even if they weren't Philip's, they belonged to Alexander's time. So while the vast empire created by Alexander no longer exists, we still have many of the beautiful treasures that were created when that young man was the most important person of the Western world.

. . . gold wreath of oak leaves and acorns. The oak tree was the sacred tree of Zeus, who was the most important god in ancient Greece.

Put on a pair of foxy earphones and hear sounds the way a fennec does.

A ZOO JUST FOR YOU

How does it feel to burrow like a prairie dog? To hear like a fox? To crawl like a snail? To move like a spider on a web?

You can learn the answers to these and many other questions about animals if you visit the new Children's Zoo at the Bronx Zoo, in New York City. And you can learn not just by looking at the animals but by sharing some of their activities. You can go through an underground burrow, pop your head up through a hole in the earth, and perhaps find yourself face to face with a prairie dog who's doing the same thing. You can put on a pair of foxy earphones and hear the sounds around you the way a fennec does. You can get inside a special snail shell and crawl at a snail's pace. And you can climb a huge spiderweb made of rope.

The new Children's Zoo is divided into five areas. Each of the first four is an example

of a different kind of wild place: the woodland edge, the marsh, the forest, and the desert. Each shows some of the typical animals and plants that you would find in such a place in the wild. In addition, each area gives examples of the ways animals do different things.

• In the woodland edge, you'll learn about animal homes. That's where you'll find the prairie-dog burrows and the spiderweb. You can also look for some raccoons in a hollow log—and there's another hollow log for *you* to crawl through, just to see what it's like.

• In the marsh, you'll learn how animals move—by swimming, flying, crawling, jumping. That's where the special snail shell is. There's also a glass-walled pond that lets you see ducks swimming and diving, with their feet at your eye level. You can even test your jumping ability against a bullfrog's.

Get inside a special snail shell and crawl at a snail's pace.

• The forest area shows how animals defend themselves—with spines (a porcupine), with nasty smells (a skunk), with stings (a hornet), by being hard to see (an insect called a walking stick, which looks just like a stick that walks), by simply running away (a lizard).

• The desert area tells about animal senses—smell, taste, touch, hearing, and sight. There you'll find Freddie the Fennec, the official mascot of the Children's Zoo. Freddie is a small, sand-colored desert fox with very big, sharp ears. You'll also find the earphones shaped just like his ears.

• The fifth area has familiar domestic animals that you can pet and feed—goats, sheep, pigs, rabbits, ducks, geese, a pony, and a donkey. In the nursery, you'll see animals that have just been born.

The Children's Zoo has been created especially for you. It's a great place to have fun while learning about the creatures that share our planet with us.

The 13th-century castle at Segovia, Spain, casts a spell of legend and romance.

ONCE UPON A CASTLE

Castles make us think of fairy tales and enchanted lands. They bring to mind romantic stories of bold knights, fair maidens, and legendary kings and queens. But in fact, most castles were not romantic at all. They were built for defense in a violent age, and life in them was harsh by today's standards.

The castles you are probably most familiar with were built in Europe during the Middle Ages. But at different times in history, castles were built in many places—in the Middle East and the Far East as well as in Europe. Like forts, they defended strategic places such as mountain passes and river crossings. But while both forts and castles housed troops, a castle was also the home of its owner—a king or a lord.

EARLY EUROPEAN CASTLES

Castles developed along with feudal systems. In these systems, powerful lords owned large areas of land, called fiefs. A lord might serve a king, but he was master of his fief. To help him defend his fief—from his neighbors as well as from foreign raiders—he could call on the men who were under his rule: his vassals. And a lord could build castles. A lesser lord might rule his fief from one castle. But the more powerful lords scattered castles throughout their lands, and they moved with their families from one castle to the next.

Motte-and-Bailey Castles. Early European castles were modeled on the forts of the Roman Empire. But they were a far cry from the solid walls and towers of the Romans. A typical castle of the year 1000 was built of earth and wood, in a form called motte and bailey.

The outer defense of a motte-and-bailey castle was a deep ditch, or moat, often filled with water. Usually, the moat took the form of a figure eight. In one half of the eight, the *motte*—a tall mound of earth—would be raised. On top of the mound the lord would build a wooden tower, in which he lived. A stockade of pointed logs surrounded it.

A long, sloping bridge led down from the motte and across the moat to the other half of the eight, the *bailey*. The bailey was simply a flat area enclosed by a wooden stockade, with stables and other buildings for work and storage. The main entrance to the castle was usually at the end of the bailey farthest from the motte. There, a drawbridge could be lowered to admit friendly visitors.

Motte-and-bailey castles were most common in England and France, but they were built in other parts of Europe as well. They could be put up quickly and cheaply. But the wood they were built of could rot or burn or be smashed by attackers.

The solution to these problems was the stone castle. Some stone castles were built in France in the early 1000's. Because of the great weight of the stone, they stood on natural hills or level ground, rather than on artificial mounds.

When the Normans conquered England in 1066, they established their rule by quickly putting up motte-and-bailey castles everywhere. But by the 1100's, they were replacing these early castles with stone ones. One of the first stone castles to be built in England was the White Tower of the Tower of London, so called because it was painted white. It was begun in 1078.

Norman Castles. A typical Norman castle was enclosed by a stone wall, called a *curtain wall,* and ringed by a moat. The entrance to the castle—across a drawbridge—was defended by a stone gatehouse. And the gate itself could be blocked with a heavy iron grill called a *portcullis,* which dropped into place from above.

The massive curtain wall was thickest at the base, to withstand battering rams and to make it hard for attackers to sap (collapse by removing the base stones). Towers were placed at intervals along the wall.

The area inside the curtain wall was often divided by another wall, to form an inner and an outer bailey. In the outer bailey were barns and other buildings, a garden, and an exercise yard for the men-at-arms. The inner bailey contained storehouses and kitchen buildings, and perhaps a chapel. But its main feature was the *keep,* or *donjon*—a massive square tower in which the lord and his family lived.

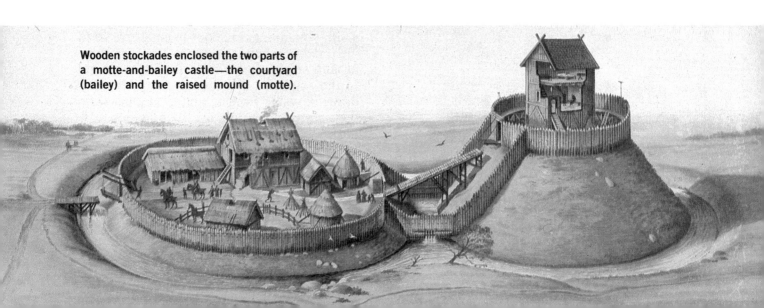

Wooden stockades enclosed the two parts of a motte-and-bailey castle—the courtyard (bailey) and the raised mound (motte).

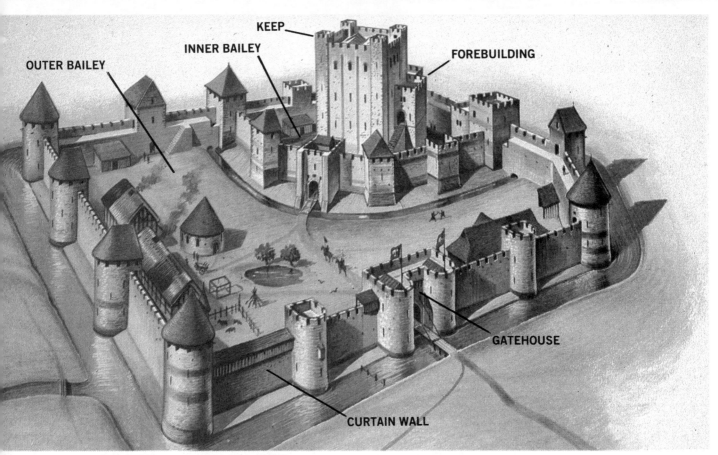

KEEP

INNER BAILEY

FOREBUILDING

OUTER BAILEY

GATEHOUSE

CURTAIN WALL

A typical Norman castle of the 1100's.

The keep was uncomfortable—cold, damp, and drafty. The ground floor was used for storage. The entrance, at the second floor, was reached by a flight of stone steps that led to a small side tower called the forebuilding. The second floor provided living quarters for the castle's garrison.

The lord's quarters were on the third floor. Most of this floor was taken up by the Great Hall, a large room where meals were served and official business was carried on.

The lord's *solar,* where he received important visitors and often slept, was here, too. Other sleeping chambers were on the fourth and final floor. *Garderobes,* or bathrooms, were cut into the thick stone walls of the keep. They were simply latrines that emptied into the moat.

Suppose you could go back to the 1100's and visit a Norman castle. What would it be like?

LIFE IN A NORMAN CASTLE

Your first impression might be one of bustling activity. As you enter the outer bailey, soldiers are practicing with long, heavy swords in the exercise yard. The sound of a smith's hammer rings out from a low building nearby, where the armorer is repairing a broken shield. Some men are adding thatch to the roof of a storehouse. A stableboy is drawing water from a well in the center of the court, and others are rubbing down the horses of a recently returned hunting party. In a pen beyond the stable, pigs grunt and squeal. Geese and chickens scatter as you walk through to the inner bailey.

Here, delicious smells pour from the kitchen building. Eating and drinking are an important form of entertainment in the castle, and today a feast is being prepared. Cooks and helpers scurry this way and that in the kitchen. Great cauldrons of stew bubble over the fire, and chickens are roasting on a spit. One cook makes pastry for a meat pie. And in one corner, a lowly scullion cleans cups and wooden platters. In the buttery, next to the kitchen, the butler rolls out a cask of ale to be tapped.

You pass by and go up the stairs to the keep, pausing to let your eyes adjust to the dim light. Then you go up a narrow spiral stairway to the Great Hall. This is a huge room, with a high wooden ceiling. Tapestries hang on the stone walls, and rushes are strewn on the floor. The few narrow windows and the fire burning in the great fireplace do little to dispel the darkness or the chill.

Near the fire, two squires are having a game of tables, which is rather like backgammon. Near them, the lady of the castle is giving instructions to a seamstress. Servants are moving rough wooden tables and benches into place for the feast. The lord's table is on the dais, a raised platform at one end of the hall. His is the only chair.

Off the Great Hall is the solar, the lord's private room. There the lord is conferring with his steward, who is in charge of managing the estate. The lord sits on the bed while the steward, standing, goes over a list of rents due from tenant farmers. In comparison to the rest of the castle, this room seems bright and comfortable. A large arched window looks out over the bailey. The walls are covered with rich hangings, and there are fur throws on the floor. Two hunting dogs sprawl in front of the solar's large hooded fireplace.

On another visit, you might find the lord in the Great Hall, hearing the complaints of his vassals and administering justice. Or he might be riding out to hunt or hearing services in the chapel next to the keep. But whenever the lord is at the castle, the staff —anywhere from a dozen to a hundred people—will be hard at work. Servants bring in food from surrounding farms, carry wood for fires, do laundry and mending, heat water for

baths, bake bread, brew ale, make medicines, and carry out dozens of other household chores. Clerks write letters and keep accounts. The chapel priest gives lessons to the lord's children. Traveling minstrels may be on hand to provide entertainment.

If the lord's household is large, food supplies will be used up in a few weeks. The moat will be fouled with wastes. Then the lord and most of his retainers will move on to another of his castles. The permanent staff—a small garrison of men-at-arms and a few servants—will stay behind and clean up.

Your visit would be quite different if you found the castle under attack. The lord's enemies would try to take the castle by laying siege to it. They would surround the castle to cut off its supplies. Then they would move toward the walls under the cover of wooden screens and begin to attack the castle at all points.

Some enemy soldiers would begin to fill in a section of the moat so that a tall wooden tower called a *belfrey* could be rolled up to the walls. If they succeeded, archers could shoot down into the bailey from the top of

Soldiers manned the walls when the castle was attacked.

the belfrey. Soldiers might even be able to enter the castle by dropping a bridge across to the top of the wall. Or the attackers might bring across a battering ram and begin to pound on the main gate or the walls.

Others would set wooden bridges across the moat and try to scale the walls with ladders. Meanwhile, catapults would send their missiles soaring over the walls and raining down into the bailey—spears, stones, and flammable liquid called Greek fire.

Many castles were so bristling with defenses that they might well withstand such an onslaught. Defenders could shoot arrows through narrow slits, called *loopholes,* in the tower walls. They could also defend the castle from the wall-walk, or *allure.* This was a narrow walkway near the top of the wall. Archers could shoot from evenly spaced gaps, called *crenels,* at the top of the wall. And when the castle was attacked, wooden galleries called *hoardings* were hung out over the walls. Defenders stood in the hoardings and dropped stones and boiling liquids down on the attackers.

Of course, any castle could be taken if the attackers waited long enough. The defenders would run out of food and be forced to surrender or starve. But often the attackers couldn't wait. Under the feudal system, men-at-arms were usually required to serve their lords for a period of only 40 days. If the castle hadn't surrendered in that time, the attacking army was likely to disband and go home.

DIFFERENT CASTLE DESIGNS

Feudal society was common to most of Europe in the Middle Ages, and so was the basic castle design. But there were many variations. In Germany and some other parts of Europe, the keep was a place of refuge when the castle was attacked, but the lord and his family lived in a low building next to it in times of peace. Such keeps were taller and slimmer than the Norman ones, and the residences were more spacious.

In France, some keeps were made up of separate towers. These towers were linked by walls to enclose a courtyard. The French were also the first in Europe to replace wooden hoardings with permanent stone galleries called *machicolations.*

As time went on, there were many other changes in castle design. Some came about as a result of the Crusades, which began in the 11th century and continued into the 13th century. When the European Crusaders traveled to the Middle East, they saw different kinds of defenses, and they brought back new ideas.

One of the most important ideas was that of the concentric castle. The main feature of a concentric castle was an extra ring of walls. Attackers who managed to break through the outer ring would be faced with a second ring, taller than the first. And they would be trapped in the open space between.

Another important change was the round keep. The corners of the square keep had always been a weak point because it was fairly easy for attackers to pry out a cornerstone and bring the keep down. A round keep was much more difficult to sap.

The main gate was strengthened by the addition of a gatehouse, called a *barbican,* that stood like an island in the moat. Attackers would have to take the barbican before they assailed the main gate. And the barbican was like a miniature castle. It had two portcullises, and stones could be dropped on intruders through *murder-holes* in the ceiling of the main passage.

As the outer defenses became stronger, the keep became less important. In later castles, the lord and his family often lived in a hall that stood in the central courtyard. Instead of a single solar, the family might have a suite of rooms.

This castle in Limousin, France, was built in the 1400's. The round towers are topped with machicolations—projecting galleries supported by stone brackets. Between the brackets are holes through which defenders could drop stones.

By the late 1200's, castles had become the ultimate military defenses of their day. But gradually, they became less important. Kings became more powerful and kept large standing armies, which could wait as long as necessary for a castle to surrender. Strong rulers also put an end to much of the squabbling between local lords that had made fortress homes necessary in the early Middle Ages. Castles continued to be built in parts of Europe through the 1500's, especially in areas such as Italy where many small states fought among themselves. Many of these later castles had gunports for cannon. Or the walls might be low so that cannon could be mounted on top to fire out at attackers.

THE CASTLES OF JAPAN

Japanese castles were more elaborate—and more comfortable—than those of medieval Europe. But they had some of the same features. Many of the Japanese castles were built at the end of the 1500's, a time when local lords were fighting for control of large sections of the country. Each *daimyo*, as a lord was called, built castles to defend the territory he held.

The daimyo often picked a hilltop as the site for his castle. As in Europe, the outer line of defense was a moat, with a wall just inside it. Sometimes this outer wall was built of grass-covered earth, but more often it was faced with massive stones. Built to withstand earthquakes as well as enemies, some walls were 50 feet (15 meters) thick at the base. On top was a parapet, built of wood, clay, and plaster and roofed with tile. Defenders on the parapet could shoot arrows through loopholes, or they could drop stones and boiling water through chutes called *ishiotoshi*. Towers, one to three stories tall, stood at the corners of the wall.

Usually the moat was crossed by a permanent bridge or causeway, rather than a drawbridge. Gates were often complicated. For example, visitors might enter through an outer gate into a small court. Then they would turn at right angles to pass through a second, larger gate, which was defended by a gatehouse.

Beyond the gatehouse was a maze of courtyards. They were arranged so that if one courtyard fell to attackers, the rest could still be defended. The courtyards were often beautifully landscaped, and their gardens

helped the defense. Evergreens grew up to hide the walls, so that attackers could not see what the defenders were up to. The trees also provided an extra screen against enemy arrows. And when the castle was under siege, oak and bamboo from the gardens could be used for spear and arrow shafts, and garden pools provided an extra source of water.

The chief retainers and *samurai* (men-at-arms) lived in the inner courtyards. In the central courtyard, on the highest ground, were the keep and the palace of the daimyo. The keep, or *tenshu-kaku*, was three to seven stories tall, wider at the base than at the top. Many keeps were painted black. Like the other castle buildings, the keep had a tile roof with curved gables. A pair of mythical dolphins called *sachi* were placed at each end of the ridgepole as a charm against evil.

The keep was the castle's chief command

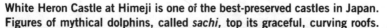

White Heron Castle at Himeji is one of the best-preserved castles in Japan. Figures of mythical dolphins, called *sachi,* top its graceful, curving roofs.

post and its final line of defense. Sometimes a courtyard near it was set aside for the purpose of committing suicide, in the event the castle was taken. In times of siege, the daimyo and his retainers lived in the keep.

Most of the time, the daimyo lived in the palace. This building might be decorated with elaborate carvings and fine works of art. The wood floors were often laid in a pattern called *uguisu-bari,* or nightingale boarding, so that they would make noise when people walked on them. This made it difficult for enemies to sneak into the palace at night.

By the early 1600's, most of Japan had been united under a *shogun,* or military ruler. The daimyos became less important. Gradually their castles were abandoned and fell into disrepair.

RUINS AND RESTORATIONS

In Europe, too, the end of the feudal system made castles obsolete. Nobles were less interested in defense and more interested in comfort. They moved out of their damp castles and into stately manors, or they remodeled the castles with an eye to comfort. It wasn't until the 1800's that castles took on the romantic appeal they have today.

By then, most of the medieval castles were crumbling into ruins. Many were restored—sometimes accurately, sometimes fancifully. Wealthy people built homes that looked like castles, with crenellated rooflines and narrow slits of windows.

What may be the most lavish imitation castle anywhere is Neuschwanstein Castle, built by Ludwig II, king of Bavaria, in the late 1800's. Ludwig got so carried away with this castle—and spent such vast sums of money on it—that the Bavarian Government declared him insane and deposed him. Neuschwanstein is perched on a spur of rock, with the Alps towering behind it and a lake at its feet. Its white spires and towers and beautifully furnished interior are nothing like the rough, damp castles of earlier days.

Many restored castles are open to the public, in Japan as well as in Europe. If you visit one, you can step into the pages of history and see what life was like in feudal times. But if you visit Neuschwanstein, you can step straight into a fairy tale.

Neuschwanstein Castle, in the Bavarian Alps, may be one of the most fanciful castles ever built.

WHAT DO YOU MEAN BY THAT?

Did you spill the beans? Are you in hot water? Do you have feet of clay?

These questions might not make sense to someone who is not very familiar with the English language. That's because they contain idioms—expressions with special meanings that can't be figured out from the individual words in them. Like many idioms, these expressions rose out of stories and situations that are hundreds and sometimes thousands of years old. Today the stories and situations are often forgotten, but the idioms live on.

SPILL THE BEANS

You "spill the beans" when you tell a secret to someone who's not supposed to know. This idiom goes back to ancient Greece. The Greeks had secret societies that were like very exclusive clubs. When someone wanted to join one of these societies, the members would vote. Each member would put a bean into a pottery jar—a white bean for a "yes" vote, a brown bean for a "no" vote. The vote was kept secret so that the person's feelings wouldn't be hurt if there were a lot of brown beans. Only the leaders were supposed to look in the jar. But sometimes a member would knock the jar over and spill the beans—and the secret would be out.

PULL THE WOOL OVER SOMEONE'S EYES

To "pull the wool over someone's eyes" is to fool that person. This idiom is thought to date from the 1700's, when fashionable gentlemen wore elaborate wigs. The human or animal hair that was used to make the wigs was generally called wool. Practical jokers (and sometimes thieves, too) would sneak up behind a gentleman and tip his wig down over his eyes, so that he couldn't see. The joker would run off laughing—but the thief would steal the gentleman's money!

IN HOT WATER

When you're "in hot water," you're in trouble. This expression is thought to have come from a test that was used hundreds of years ago to show innocence or guilt. A person accused of a crime would be told to reach into a pot of boiling water. People were judged guilty if they were burned (which, of course, they always were).

COLD SHOULDER

If you get the "cold shoulder" from someone, you've been snubbed and treated rudely. In this expression, "shoulder" refers to a cut of meat for roasting, not a part of the rude person's body. The saying is thought to have originated in medieval times, when it was the custom for nobles to offer a hot meal and a bed to any weary traveler who knocked on the castle gate. But unwelcome travelers would be offered only a meal of leftovers —perhaps a few slices from a cold shoulder of mutton—in the hope that they would go away.

FEET OF CLAY

"Feet of clay" are a weakness. This idiom comes from the Old Testament of the Bible. In the Book of Daniel, King Nebuchadnezzar dreams of a statue with a head made of gold, chest and arms of silver, stomach and thighs of brass, legs of iron, and feet partly of iron and partly of clay. A stone strikes the feet, and the whole statue shatters. Daniel interprets the dream to mean the decline of the King's realm. Nowadays, the expression is used to refer to a weak point in the character of a person who is otherwise strong.

The Stolen Crown
A FAIRY TALE FROM ITALY

Early one morning in May, the King of Naples and his Royal Wizard went hunting. At midday they stopped for a light lunch of apricots and oranges, and the King, before lying down to take a nap, gave his royal crown to the Wizard for safekeeping.

The Wizard put the crown in his saddlebag and himself lay down to nap.

An hour or so later the King awoke. Before mounting his horse to continue the hunt, he called for his crown. The Wizard reached into his saddlebag and felt around. Then he opened the bag wide—but found no crown. He could see the King was getting impatient, but he hemmed and hawed. "Well, Sire, I don't know how to tell you this, but . . . your crown is . . . gone!"

"Gone?" cried the King. "GONE?"

"Y-yes, Sire," quavered the Wizard.

"Well, Royal Wizard," snapped the King, "you lost it—YOU find it!" And he yanked his horse around and galloped back to his palace.

The Wizard followed, wondering desperately how he was going to find the King's crown. He knew that, at the very least, he'd be out of a job if he failed.

Now the King of Naples had three sons, and one of the Wizard's duties was to give them their lessons. He taught them Latin grammar and multiplication tables, and he often quoted proverbs to them, to teach them to be clever. "Fortune favors the brave," he would say, or, "A rolling stone gathers no moss."

This particular afternoon, however, the three princes found that their teacher wasn't even bothering to correct Alfonso when he stumbled over eleven-times-twelve.

The boys exchanged glances, and the eldest, Prince Pietro, finally asked, "Good teacher, what is wrong?"

The Wizard heaved a great sigh and explained about the King's missing crown. He apologized for not paying attention in class, but said he was having a hard time deciding how to find the King's crown.

"There, now, friend Wizard," comforted Prince Luigi. "We'll help you get the crown back. But 'time marches on,' as you always say, so let's get busy."

The boys put away their schoolwork, and the Wizard thumbed through his dusty book of spells until he came to one that he thought would be just the ticket for finding a lost crown. The Wizard took a pellet of lead and put it in a pan, which he set on a tripod over a flame. While the lead heated, he filled a glass bottle with cold water.

When the lead had melted, the Wizard poured it into the cold water. Slowly the swirling droplets condensed into a shape. The Wizard gasped.

"What's wrong, good teacher?" asked Prince Alfonso.

"Oh, evil day!" groaned the Wizard. "Now I will surely lose my job!"

"See here, Wizard," demanded Prince Pietro, who was old enough to demand things. "Stop worrying about your job. What about my father's crown?"

So the Wizard explained that the shape formed by the drop of lead was that of Bruttina, a beautiful but very powerful witch who lived in a magic grotto in the shadow of Mount Vesuvius.

"It is she who has stolen your father's crown," revealed the Wizard. "I am powerless against her magic."

"Well, we can't give up before we've begun," said Prince Luigi, who, although he was the youngest, was also the most sensible of the princes. "Even if we fail, we must at least try to get Father's crown back."

The Royal Wizard had little hope that three youngsters who didn't even know their "times-twelves" could do anything against Bruttina, but he was proud of their courage. So he gave them directions to Bruttina's grotto and told them to be careful.

The three young princes set off on their white mules for the slopes of Vesuvius. As they traveled, they thought up plan after plan for getting the crown away from Bruttina, but every plan had a flaw.

Nevertheless, counting on inspiration and recalling their teacher's advice, "Stop to think and lose the opportunity," they rode on. At last they reached the entrance to Bruttina's grotto.

Cautiously, Prince Pietro peeked through the gate. Inside he saw a wondrous garden, full of giant flowers. But this was no ordinary garden, for all the flowers were made

of precious jewels—ruby and diamond blooms, with emerald leaves. Even though they lived in a royal palace, the three princes had never seen such beautiful treasures.

Then Prince Luigi piped up. "It looks like Bruttina has all the riches she could want, but there's one thing I bet she doesn't get very often . . ."

The boys hopped back on their royal mules and set off the way they had come. Soon they returned, each prince holding a huge bouquet of flowers. They tied the mules to a pear tree outside Bruttina's gate and boldly walked up to her door. The plan was to woo the witch with flowers and persuade her to return their father's crown.

Prince Pietro knocked at the door, which was also decorated with precious gems. No answer. Then Prince Alfonso stepped up

and rapped loudly with the golden knocker. Still no answer.

Then sensible Prince Luigi stepped forward. "Yoo-hoo!" he called. "Is anyone home?"

"No!" came the reply.

"But we have come all the way from the King, with gifts for the most beautiful witch in the world," said Luigi, figuring flattery might get him somewhere.

Sure enough, Bruttina was vain, not to mention curious. "Then come in," she called, "for those gifts couldn't be for anyone but me."

The boys walked down a jeweled hallway

to the witch's room. Each held his bouquet of flowers in front of him, to make the best possible first impression.

Bruttina turned away from her mirror, where she was admiring her new crown. As soon as she saw the boys, she screeched, "FLOWERS! You fools! Get out!"

"B-but, Your Witchiness," protested Alfonso, "we only brought you three simple bouquets."

"I can't sta . . . aahh . . . aaahhh . . . aaaaCHOOOO!" she sneezed. Soon the wretched witch couldn't even talk because of all her sneezing.

Luigi was as quick-witted as he was sensible. "Never let it be said that we failed to take advantage of an opportunity," he said. He grabbed the crown out of Bruttina's hand and the three princes fled from the witch's jeweled garden, leaving her croaking for her guards between fits of sneezing.

"Now we know why she has no real flow-ers in her garden," chuckled Pietro to his brothers. They rode away from Vesuvius laughing, remembering the sight of the witch's fits of sneezing.

As they neared the palace, they saw the Royal Wizard pacing in the courtyard, wringing his hands. When he recognized the three princes, his relief knew no bounds.

"Thank heaven you're back safe," he said. "How did you fare?"

Pietro held up the King's golden crown, and its jewels sparkled in the sun.

So not only did the King of Naples get his crown back, but his three sons became known far and wide for their cleverness. And Bruttina shut herself away in her grotto, ashamed that she had been beaten by three boys who didn't even know their "times-twelves" yet.

And the Wizard? Why, he became even more famous than his pupils, for wasn't it he who had taught them all they knew?

THE HEART OF THE MATTER

The most popular exhibit at the Franklin Institute in Philadelphia, Pennsylvania, is a human heart. But it's no ordinary heart. It's 125,000 times the size of a real heart. It's so big that you can walk through it, pretending that you are a blood cell that passes through and out of the heart.

The giant pinkish-red heart is 18 feet (5.5 meters) tall and 28 feet (8.5 meters) wide. You enter through the right atrium. This is the chamber that blood enters as it returns to the heart from the arms, legs, head, and most other parts of the body.

From the right atrium, you pass through a narrow opening into the right ventricle. This is the chamber that pumps blood to the lungs. From there, you walk up into a hallway to see what happens in the lungs. You will learn how blood releases carbon dioxide and picks up oxygen in the lungs. Then, just like a blood cell, you return to the heart.

Now you move on to the left side of the heart. You enter the left atrium and then go into the left ventricle. The left ventricle is the most muscular part of the heart. It pumps blood to every part of the body except the lungs. Blood leaves the left ventricle through a very large blood vessel called the aorta. This is the same way that visitors leave the Franklin Institute heart—through a giant aorta.

As you look back, you can see the openings to the coronary arteries. These first branches of the aorta go to the walls of the heart itself. The muscles that make up the walls of the heart need a constant supply of food and oxygen.

Near the giant heart is an exhibit that shows how hard the heart works as it continuously supplies blood to all parts of the body. The exhibit has a hand pump that allows you to compare your hand muscles to the heart muscles. Attached to the hand pump is a scale that shows how much body weight your hand muscles could support if they were pumping blood. Some people's hand muscles can keep up with the heart—for a short time. But the hand muscles soon tire, while the heart muscles keep pumping. They pump every second of your life.

As you walk through this popular exhibit at the Franklin Institute, you can pretend that you are a blood cell passing through a human heart.

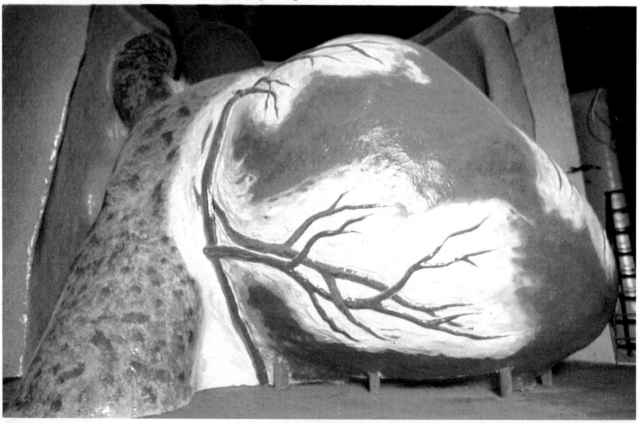

DID YOU KNOW...

The symbol of Valentine's Day is a human heart. But the heart used on Valentine's Day doesn't look like a healthy heart. It looks like a very sick heart. If it were a healthy heart, the left side would be bigger than the right side.

Big people have bigger hearts than small people. The normal weight of a human heart is about 0.5 percent of the total body weight. For example, if you weigh 100 pounds (45 kilograms), your heart weighs about a half pound (0.2 kilograms).

Athletes have heavier hearts and stronger heart muscles than people who do not exercise a lot. This is true for animals, too. A very active dog has a larger, stronger heart than a lazy dog.

Different people have different heart rates. Athletes usually have lower heart rates than nonathletes. Their hearts use fewer beats to pump the same amount of blood.

The heart rate of the average person is about 72 beats per minute. Many athletes, especially those who are long-distance runners or swimmers, have heart rates of about 45 beats per minute.

The heart rate slows down when you sleep. It speeds up when you get excited or angry. It also speeds up when you exercise.

At an average rate of 72 beats per minute, the heart contracts (beats) about 4,320 times in one hour, about 103,680 times in one day, and about 37,843,200 times in one year.

Small hearts beat faster than big hearts. A baby's heart beats faster than an adult's heart.

The shrew is the smallest mammal on earth. It has a heart rate of 1,000 beats per minute. The blue whale, the largest animal on earth, has a rate of only 5 or 6 beats per minute.

Each time the heart beats, blood is pumped out of the heart. In one minute, at least 4 quarts (3.8 liters) of blood leave the heart. The blood travels through 60,000 miles (96,500 kilometers) of blood vessels. If all your blood vessels were placed end to end, they would form a tube more than long enough to circle the world twice.

Many chemicals affect the heart rate. Nicotine, a chemical in cigarettes, increases the heart rate. So does caffeine, which is found in coffee, tea, and many soft drinks.

Temperature affects the heart rate. The heart beats faster on warm days than on cold days.

Noise increases the heart rate. The greater the noise, the greater the increase. This is true even if you are sleeping.

THE ROYAL WEDDING

"Here is the stuff of which fairy tales are made: the Prince and Princess on their wedding day. But fairy tales usually end at this point with the simple phrase, 'They lived happily ever after.' This may be because fairy stories regard marriage as an anticlimax after the romance of courtship.

"This is not the Christian view. Our faith sees the wedding day not as the place of arrival but the place where the adventure really begins."

These words were spoken by the Most Reverend Robert Runcie, the Archbishop of Canterbury, at the year's most magnificent wedding. It was the wedding of 32-year-old Prince Charles, heir to the British throne, and 20-year-old Lady Diana Spencer.

The wedding took place in London on July 29, 1981—a day that blazed with glamour and pageantry and was filled with cheers and laughter. It was the climax of six months of excitement that had begun in February, when Charles gave Diana a brilliant sapphire and diamond ring and the couple announced their engagement.

More than 2,500 guests filled high-domed St. Paul's Cathedral, the beautiful, 300-year-old church where the wedding took place. There were kings and queens from other countries, heads of state, and other international figures. Other guests included Charles's former schoolteachers, Diana's former roommates, members of the household staffs at the royal palaces, and sailors from the naval ship that Charles had once commanded.

Outside, under sunny skies, hundreds of thousands of flag-waving spectators lined the streets between St. Paul's and Buckingham Palace, the home of the royal family. Some had waited all night to catch a glimpse of the Prince and his bride. And around the world, 700,000,000 people watched the ceremony on television.

About 10 A.M., the first of the eleven antique horse-drawn carriages that formed the wedding procession clattered through the gates of Buckingham Palace. The carriages were escorted by the royal household cavalry, in gleaming breastplates and plumed helmets. The Welsh guards, in scarlet coats and tall fur hats, lined the route. One coach carried Queen Elizabeth II and Prince Philip, the parents of Prince Charles. Later, Prince Charles, looking dignified and handsome in his Royal Navy uniform, passed through the cheering crowd. Finally, in a glass coach, came Lady Diana and her father.

The crowd oohed and aahed as Lady Diana stepped from the carriage and walked up the steps of the church. Her pale ivory taffeta gown was made of silk from the only silk farm in England, hand-embroidered with pearls, sequins, and lace. It had a full skirt, a fitted bodice, and a romantic curving neckline. On her head, Lady Diana wore a diamond tiara. And a 25-foot (7.5-meter) train swept behind her as her father led her up the aisle. Five bridesmaids and two pages accompanied them.

At the altar were the groom and his two "supporters"—his brothers Prince Andrew and Prince Edward. Throughout the ceremony, which lasted more than an hour, music filled the cathedral. And when the Archbishop pronounced the couple man and wife, Prince Charles placed a ring of Welsh gold on the third finger of the bride's left hand, and she became Diana, Princess of Wales.

After the ceremony, the royal family returned to Buckingham Palace. Charles and Diana appeared on the palace balcony, together with their parents and members of the wedding party. As the crowd below chanted, "Kiss her, kiss her," Charles turned to his bride and gave her a gentle kiss. The happy cheers of the watching crowd mingled with the sounds of trumpets and hundreds of ringing church bells.

After a wedding breakfast that included lobster, lamb, champagne, and wedding fruitcake, the Prince and Princess left on their honeymoon. The carriage that carried them away from the palace surprised and delighted everyone—the Prince's brothers had decorated it with a big bunch of heart-shaped balloons and a hand-lettered sign that read, "Just Married."

The honeymooners spent two days at a secluded country estate in southern England. Then they flew to Gibraltar, where they boarded the royal yacht, *Britannia*, for a two-week cruise of the Mediterranean.

After their return to England, they gradually took up their duties as Prince and Prin-

Diana's engagement ring and Charles's crest ring.

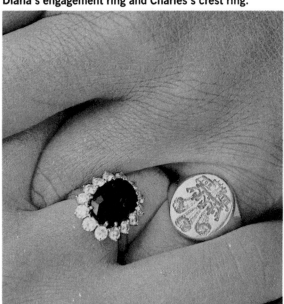

Eleven antique horse-drawn carriages formed the wedding procession to St. Paul's Cathedral. One coach carried Queen Elizabeth II and Prince Philip.

cess. Many of these are ceremonial—opening parks, planting commemorative trees, and touring factories. They will also travel to other countries as goodwill ambassadors. Wherever they are, whatever they do, Charles and Diana are expected to set an example for the British. This puts limits on what they can do and say. As Charles's sister, Princess Anne, once said: "You are always a bit on your guard. You know that because you're royal, anything you say might be given extra significance."

Like most royals, Charles and Diana will divide their time between a number of places. They have apartments in at least seven royal residences. When in London, they will live in Kensington Palace. But their own home is Highgrove, an estate in the rolling Cotswold Hills, west of London. Highgrove is rather small by royal standards. It has nine bedrooms, six bathrooms, and four large reception rooms. One wing holds a children's nursery. This wing may have a tenant soon—in November, Charles and Diana announced that their first child was expected in June, 1982.

Charles and Diana received thousands of wedding gifts—silver and crystal bowls, candlesticks, beds, kitchen utensils, cushions, and a bedspread hand-knitted by Queen Mata'aho of Tonga. The couple even received a ton of peat, a nickel-silvered mousetrap, and an herb garden for Highgrove. But the most precious gift was the love and best wishes of people everywhere.

Reverend Runcie expressed it this way: "However long they live may they always know that when they pledged themselves to each other before the altar of God they were surrounded and supported not by mere spectators, but by the sincere affection and active prayer of millions of friends."

PRINCE CHARLES

Charles Philip Arthur George has many titles: Prince of Wales and Earl of Chester, Duke of Cornwall, Duke of Rothesay, Earl of Carrick and Baron of Renfrew, Lord of the Isles and Great Steward of Scotland. Someday he will have one of the grandest titles of all—King of England.

Charles was born on November 14, 1948. He is the oldest of the four children of Queen Elizabeth II and Prince Philip. He is the first Prince of Wales in history to be educated at a regular school, rather than by private tutors, and the first to graduate from a university. He served as an officer in both the Royal Air Force and the Royal Navy. He is a pilot who has flown helicopters, propeller planes, and jets. He has also trained as a commando, parachute jumper, and frogman. Charles's love of outdoor activities is well known. His favorite sports include polo, riding, skiing, and salmon fishing. He also loves classical music and plays the cello.

The motto of the Prince of Wales is "I serve." Charles takes this seriously. He assists with the duties of the royal family, keeps informed about politics, and meets with government leaders, in addition to managing his own vast property holdings. As one historian said, "He's the right sort of person for a modern monarch—hard working, buoyant and cheerful, with a deep sense of purpose."

DIANA, PRINCESS OF WALES

Diana Frances Spencer became the first English woman to marry an heir to the throne in more than 300 years. She was born on July 1, 1961, the daughter of the eighth Earl Spencer and his first wife, Frances. Although she is not of royal birth, she is related to royalty—the Spencers trace their lineage to the Stuart kings of England. It could be said that Charles married the girl next door. Diana spent her childhood at Park House in Sandringham, on the royal family's estate. Her playmates included Charles's brothers, Prince Andrew and Prince Edward, who are about her age. She knew the Queen well enough to call her "Aunt Lilibet."

When she was young, Diana had a private tutor. Later, she attended a boarding school and a finishing school in Switzerland. Like Charles, Diana loves music, the outdoors, and animals. She also loves children. After completing school, she worked for an American couple, caring for their young child. Later, she worked in a kindergarten in London.

Life as the wife of the future King of England will be very different from life as a commoner. Diana must address her husband as "Sir" in public. She must walk one step behind him. She cannot go anywhere unannounced—not even to see friends or to go shopping. But she will enjoy a life of great wealth and luxury with the man she loves.

The Grouch

Barbershop Quartet

LET'S FACE IT

Look closely. All these "faces" aren't faces at all. They are pieces of nature. The Barbershop Quartet singers are markings on a butterfly wing. The Grouch with the spiky hair is a common weed called a teasel. Curious Fish is part of a moth wing. A japonica shrub and an icicle created Runny Nose.

Runny Nose

Curious Fish

And an orchid and droplets of water gave us
Pop-eyed Pony. If you're a good observer
and have some imagination, you can find
faces everywhere—funny ones, sad ones,
scary ones. So pick up your camera and
head outdoors. Look closely at that tree
trunk and tiger lily blossom. Is someone
looking back at you?

Pop-eyed Pony

IN LOVE WITH GARLIC

• In ancient Greece, athletes ate garlic to increase their strength.

• In ancient Rome, soldiers ate garlic to give them courage on the battlefield. They also used it to cure a long list of ailments, including snakebites, scorpion stings, and asthma.

• In 16th-century France, people wore garlic around their necks to keep vampires away and to ward off the plague.

• Medieval women believed that garlic made their skin beautiful.

• During World War I, the British used garlic as an antiseptic in treating wounded soldiers.

• Garlic has been said to prevent baldness and to cure rheumatism, leprosy, tuberculosis, and smallpox.

• In the 20th century, people are claiming that garlic helps to prevent heart attacks and that it may even cure cancer.

Since ancient times, garlic has been credited with having special mystical and medicinal powers. It has sometimes even been called the "heal-all" herb. But how much truth is there to the power of garlic? It is difficult to say for sure. Scientists have done very little research on garlic. None of the beliefs have been proved true. But on the other hand, none have been proved false.

And there *is* some evidence that garlic can fight bacteria and fungi, although not nearly as effectively as penicillin.

Most people who eat garlic today don't do so for health reasons. They eat it because they love its strong, unusual flavor.

Gilroy is a town in California where the love for garlic can readily be seen. Gilroy is the garlic capital of the United States. More garlic is grown there than anywhere else. For the past few years, the town has held an annual garlic festival, attracting thousands of people. There are bands, jugglers, and balloon rides. But the main reason people go to the festival is to smell and eat garlic. There are booths selling garlic sausage, snails in garlic butter, spaghetti with garlic sauce, and many other dishes. There is also a contest for the best garlic recipe. One year, someone entered a recipe for garlic ice cream.

There is one drawback to eating garlic—it does terrible things to your breath. So after you eat garlic, eat a few sprigs of fresh parsley. This will help fight bad breath. And it will let you enjoy garlic without chasing your friends away!

COOKING WITH GARLIC

Garlic is related to the onion, and both plants are members of the lily family. The part of the garlic that we eat is the underground bulb. The bulb is made up of pieces called cloves. An average sized bulb will have ten to twelve cloves. Each clove is enclosed in a crisp whitish skin.

To use garlic, remove the skin from the cloves. Usually, a cook minces or crushes the cloves before using them. This releases the flavorful oils. Some people use garlic powder instead of fresh garlic. Garlic powder is made by grinding up dried garlic.

Garlic is used in many dishes. And garlic bread is one of the most popular. Here is a recipe for garlic bread. It's delicious and easy to make. For one loaf, you need:

1 8-ounce loaf French or Italian bread
¼ pound butter or margarine, softened
2 cloves garlic
knife
aluminum foil

1. Remove the dry whitish skin that encloses each clove.

2. Carefully chop each clove very finely. The smaller the pieces, the better.

3. Mix the chopped garlic with the butter or margarine. Let the mixture stand at room temperature for about a half hour.

4. Preheat the oven to 350°F.

5. Cut the bread lengthwise. Spread the mixture on the inside of both the top and bottom pieces. (Optional: In addition to the garlic mixture, spread Parmesan cheese and a little paprika on the bread.)

6. Put the two pieces together. Cut the bread into serving pieces.

7. Wrap the bread in aluminum foil. It should be completely sealed in the foil.

8. Put the bread in the oven for about 15 minutes.

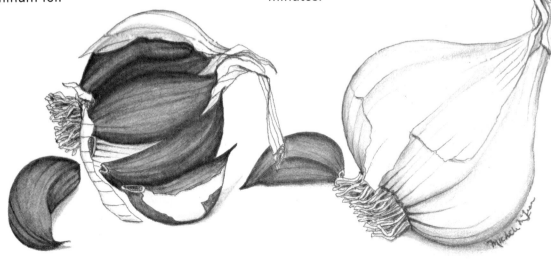

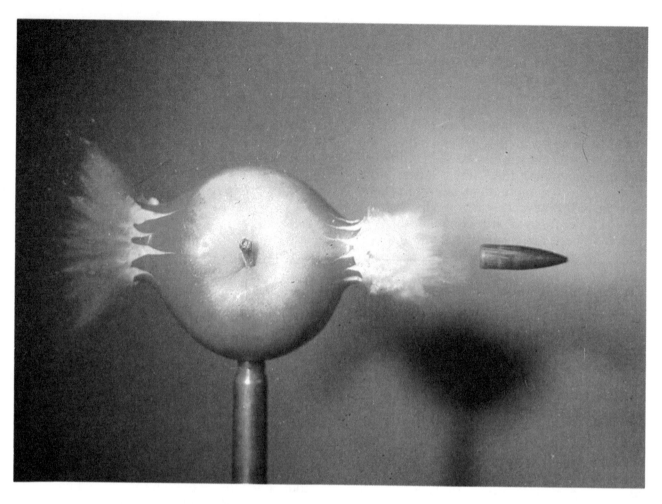

QUICKER THAN A WINK

It takes you about 1/40 of a second to wink. You may think this is an extraordinarily short period of time. Yet in 1/100,000 of a second, it's possible to snap a photograph. This type of photography is called ultra-high-speed photography. It enables us to capture motion that is too fast for the human eye to record.

With ultra-high-speed photography, motion can be frozen in time. We can see what happens when a bullet passes through an apple (*above*). The bullet is traveling at a speed of about 3,000 feet (900 meters) per second. Yet in the photo it appears to be standing still.

A jet of water is captured as a series of "flowers" connected by a thin stem of water (*left*). A picture such as this helps scientists learn how water behaves. It shows that a falling column of water—like the flow from

your kitchen faucet—quickly loses its streamlined shape. It breaks up into drops that are evenly spaced, with narrow threads of water between.

Continuous motion can be shown by rapidly making a number of exposures on one piece of film. The whole flowing motion of a tennis stroke is caught as a player hits a tennis ball (*above*). The graceful arc of a back dive can be seen in the multiple exposure at the right. Photos such as these help athletes improve their form and technique.

The term ultra-high-speed photography usually refers to exposures of 1/10,000 of a second or faster. In ordinary photography, the exposure is determined by the opening and closing of the camera's shutter. When the shutter opens, light enters the camera and makes an image on the film. In ultra-high-speed photography, exposure is determined by a flashing light. The light can flash on and off much more quickly than any shutter can open and close.

Single-Exposure "Stills": The group of photos below shows what happens when a drop of milk splashes on a plate. When the drop hits the plate, it spreads outward to form a crown. The crown collapses into a thin film of milk and a ring of tiny drops. All this happens in a fraction of a second.

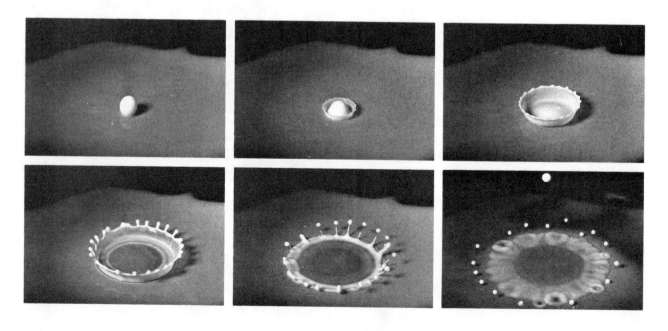

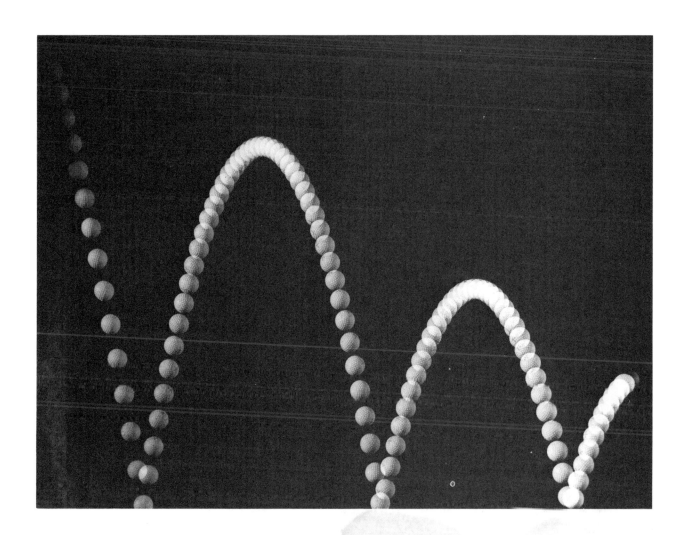

Multiple-Exposure Continuous Motion: Follow the bouncing ball above. See how the ball's movement changes as it nears the top of a bounce. The time interval between each exposure is the same. But the distance traveled by the ball changes.

WHACK!

Foxglove

WILD FLOWERS OF THE SAN JUANS

Nothing so clearly signals the end of winter than the appearance of the first wild flowers. They are the very essence of springtime. But what are wild flowers, and how are they different from the flowers that grow in our gardens?

To define a wild flower is not as easy as it seems. A wild flower to one person may be just a weed to another. However, we may say that a wild flower is any flowering plant that grows without the help of people. And from wild flowers have come all our cultivated flowers—those that we grow in gardens and greenhouses.

Camas lily

Indian paintbrush

Wild flowers are found nearly everywhere —from cracks in city sidewalks to parched desert expanses, from flat plains to rocky coasts, from mountain meadows to dark forests. They come singly, like rare treasures. Or they come in great masses, like wild splashes of paint.

On these pages are some of the wild flowers that grow in the San Juans, a group of small islands nestled in the sea north of Seattle, Washington. The islands contain many different natural habitats—bogs, marshes, lakes, creeks, open meadows, dense forests, and the seashore. And in these habitats bloom an extraordinary variety of beautiful wild flowers.

PETER D. CAPEN
Terra Mar Productions

Shooting star

Fawn lily

Long John, by Marla Cohen, 17, Park Ridge, Illinois

Peacock, by Lesa Duran, 17, Fairview Park, Ohio

YOUNG PHOTOGRAPHERS

Here's proof that something as ordinary as a bunch of colored pencils can be just as beautiful as an exotic subject—like a proud peacock. All that's needed to make the transformation is a camera and the imaginative eye of a photographer.

The photographs on these and the following pages were among the winners in the 1981 Scholastic/Kodak Photo Awards program, which was open to junior and senior high school students in the United States and Canada. The contest shows how popular photography has become with young people. And the pictures show what excellent photographers young people have become.

A Rainbow of Color, by Charlene Burroughs, 17, Burbank, California

Surreal Produce Reach, by Jeffrey Plansker, 17, Grosse Pointe Farms, Michigan

Tennis Ball,
by Peter Loisibeas, 17,
Burbank, California

Atomic Sunrise, by David Waitz, 16, Orangeburg, New York

Rooftop Overlook, by Doug Brodke, 17, Avon, Ohio

Canadian Blue Heron,
by Gerald Hare, 18,
Allison Park, Pennsylvania

Peter Pan's Growing Pains

Tinker Bell was worried about Peter Pan. He hadn't been his usual happy, carefree self lately. Nothing the little pixie did seemed to cheer him up. Peter didn't want to swim in Mermaid Lagoon or even cross swords with Captain Hook!

"It's no fun around here anymore," complained Peter. "Since Wendy and her brothers left, Never Land hasn't been the same. Maybe Wendy was right—she said I couldn't stay a boy forever."

Peter looked at Tink. "Maybe I should go back to London and grow up with my friends."

Poor little Tink! Hearing Peter talk about growing up made her ever so sad, but she gamely tried to keep up with him as he soared across the sky. "I guess he *can't* wait to grow up," she jingled sadly to herself.

It was late at night when Peter hopped through the open window of the Darling nursery. "Wendy! John! Michael! It's me— Peter Pan," he whispered. But no one answered him.

A few seconds later Tinker Bell puffed in, lighting up the darkened room. Peter saw that there were only two beds in the nursery now, one for John and one for Michael. "Oh, I remember," Peter said to Tink. "Wendy must be away at school."

Tinker Bell jingled happily, thinking that

since Wendy wasn't there, Peter might give up all this nonsense about growing up.

She didn't count on Peter's determination. "Well, that doesn't really matter," he said softly, and he glided over to John.

When he awoke, John could hardly believe his eyes. "Peter Pan! I thought I was dreaming! What are you doing here?"

"I've come to London to grow up," chuckled Peter, giving Michael a gentle shake.

"But you weren't ever going to grow up," protested Michael, rubbing his eyes.

"That's what I used to say," said Peter, "but I changed my mind. Never Land doesn't seem to be much fun anymore, so I thought coming to London and growing up would be more exciting."

John had his doubts about Peter's decision, but he kept them to himself. Michael, of course, was thrilled to have Peter come to live with them. And as John fell asleep trying

to imagine Peter Pan at school, Michael began dreaming about flying around Big Ben again.

The next morning John and Peter set off for school, leaving Michael in the nursery and Tink moping in a button box.

When they got to school, John introduced Peter to his classmates. "Oh," said Ralph, the class bully, "so you're the one John's always talking about. Well, let's see you fly," he challenged.

"Sorry, old chap," answered Peter. "I've decided to grow up, so I won't be flying anymore."

Ralph laughed a nasty laugh. "I'll bet!" he scoffed. "Well, maybe you never could fly. Maybe John made it all up."

Peter felt himself getting angry, but John stopped him. "It's not important," John said as the bell rang for class. "He's just a big bully, and it doesn't matter what he says."

Peter wasn't so sure. After all, whenever old Hook had said something mean about him or one of his friends, Peter had taught him a lesson. "Oh, well," he sighed to himself, "I can't expect things in London to be the way they were in Never Land."

That afternoon on the way home from school, Peter and John were joined by Ralph and some of his friends. "Let's play tag," suggested Ralph, with a sly look at Peter.

Now, not only was Ralph the biggest boy in his class, he was also the fastest. He figured he'd be able to tag Peter easily and embarrass him again in front of everyone.

Ralph yelled, "I'm IT," and everyone but Peter ran. Peter was so used to leaping high in the air whenever someone like Captain Hook lunged at him that he was completely taken by surprise when Ralph tagged him.

"You're IT!" jeered Ralph. Peter tried to keep his good humor and went chasing after one of the other boys. After a minute or two, he tagged John, and John was "IT."

Then Ralph did a strange thing—he slowed down so that John could tag him. It was almost as if he was trying to get tagged!

And that's exactly what Ralph was doing. He smiled a mean smile and again went after Peter. But this time, without thinking, Peter gave a tall bound and jumped right over Ralph's head.

Ralph didn't believe what he'd seen. He grabbed for Peter again, and again Peter forgot himself and flew up and hovered in the air, just out of Ralph's reach.

This time Ralph had to believe his eyes. "You . . . you *can* fly!" he choked.

All of a sudden Peter remembered—he was in London, not in Never Land. He dropped to the ground. "I'm sorry, Ralph," he apologized. "It wasn't fair of me to do that. I'll be IT."

But Ralph had tired of his little game. He was the one being shown up. So he and his friends suddenly decided they had homework to do and left Peter and John alone.

Peter hung his head. "Gosh, John," he said, "I ruined our game. I won't do it again."

"That's all right, Peter," replied John. "It was Ralph who really ruined the game. Don't worry."

The following day was Saturday, and Mr. Darling had promised to take the boys to the circus. "We'll have to hurry and get our chores done," John pointed out. Of course,

Peter had had no chores to do in Never Land, but he was a good sport, and he and John worked hard all morning long.

By noon, Peter was exhausted—all that work with his feet planted firmly on the ground. No flying the rubbish cans out to the curb, no flying in a quick circle to make a whirlwind whisk the leaves into a nice, neat pile. No flying into the air to shake the apples off the apple tree. Peter didn't think he'd ever worked so hard!

So when John went into the house to see if lunch was ready, Peter lay down on the pile of leaves. "Just a short nap," he promised himself, as his eyelids drooped.

When John came back out to the yard, he found his friend fast asleep—in the air! Even in his sleep, Peter couldn't help but fly.

John reached up and tapped on Peter's toe. Peter awoke with a start and plopped down onto the pile of leaves. After a quick lunch the boys set off for the circus, but instead of being excited, John was strangely quiet.

That night, when they were getting ready for bed, Peter asked John what was wrong. John thought for a moment, and then said, "You know, Peter, I don't think this is going to work out."

"What do you mean?" asked Peter, who wasn't sure he liked to see John looking so serious.

"You're growing up," answered John. "It just isn't right that you won't be able to fly anymore. You were *born* to fly.

"Besides," he continued, "if you grow up, what will become of Never Land?"

Peter sat down on the bed. John was right —growing up wasn't for him. It was sad to think of leaving the Darling family, but then Peter thought of all the other children who would need him.

"You're right, John," said Peter. "There should always be a Never Land. Thanks for setting me straight. I'll never forget it." He beckoned to Tinker Bell, who was so happy she jangled, and together they took off.

"Remember," shouted Peter from a cloud, "if you ever want to visit Never Land, you know how to get there."

"That's right," smiled John, waving good-bye. "Aim for the second star on the right!"

ALL WRAPPED UP

It's always fun to give presents. It's even more fun when the presents are covered in special wrappings designed by you. These pages show some of the ways you can decorate a package. Each has a theme. Some give hints to what's inside the packages. Others use pictures to say "this is especially for you!"

Before you begin, gather all the materials you want to use to decorate the package. These can include construction paper, wrapping paper, crayons, paints, markers, ribbons, yarns, lace, buttons, gold seals . . . the list is almost endless. You will also need scissors, a ruler, a compass, glue, and tape.

Begin by neatly wrapping the box. The kind of decoration will depend to some degree on the design of the wrapping paper. It's best to use solid-colored paper because it gives you more flexibility than paper with designs.

MAKE MINE VANILLA

This is a fun wrapping to use in hot summer months. The cones are triangles cut from brown construction paper. The ice cream scoops are circles of colored paper made with a compass. Can you guess all the flavors on the box?

Use markers to add nuts and sprinkles to your cones. If you wish, write a message in one or more of the ice cream scoops.

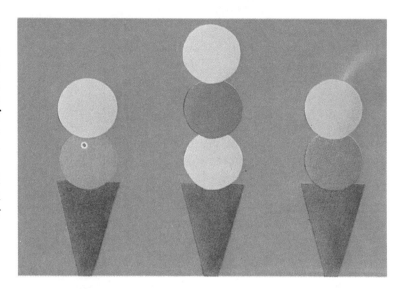

CREATIVE CANDLES

Pieces of ribbon, lace, and embroidery can be used to give an elegant appearance to a package. Cut the materials to the desired length. They can be placed on the top of the box, or they can be made long enough to wrap down the side and onto the back. Carefully determine where each will be placed, then glue it onto the box. Next, cut out flames from yellow paper. Or make the flames out of sequins, gold sprinkles, or bright red nail polish.

FUNNY FRIEND

Decorate a present with a caricature of the person who will receive the gift. Begin by cutting out a face from construction paper. This can simply be a large circle drawn with a compass. Use a different color for the shirt or blouse. Glue the face and clothing onto the box. Make hair from yarn. Glue each strand of yarn in place individually. Add a bow or hat. Next, draw on eyes, a mouth, and other facial details. Add a collar, necklace, necktie, or other decoration to the clothing.

A caricature can be made even more personal by adding objects related to the person's job or hobby. If your father likes to play baseball, make a picture of him complete with bat and ball. If your brother is a cook, add a rolling pin and a bag of flour. If your mother is a teacher, add a report card (with all A's, of course).

BON VOYAGE!

You don't have to wrap a gift in expensive paper. A brown grocery bag can be used. Newspaper can be used. Even an old road map can be used. This is an especially good idea if the gift is for someone leaving on a trip. If possible, use a map of the place the person will be visiting. If the person is touring by car, use a marker to highlight the route the person will be taking. Add a ribbon and bow for some extra color.

GARDENER'S DELIGHT

Worms are beloved by all who enjoy gardening. So if you're giving someone seeds, bulbs, garden tools, or a plant, decorate the package with Willy the Worm. Cut a wiggly body from brown paper and glue it onto the package. Add stripes and other markings to the body. Give Willy a jazzy hat and a bow tie. And add a few flowers for him to sniff.

CARD CRAZY

If you're giving a gift to someone who enjoys playing card games, decorate the wrapping with old playing cards. Or make felt cutouts of a spade, heart, diamond, and club. Use cookie cutters to help you make the design. Simply place each cookie cutter on the felt, trace its edge with pencil or chalk, then cut out the design and glue it onto your box.

WHERE WILL YOU TRAVEL?

It's time to board a spaceship for a journey into outer space. Where will the ship take you?

To answer this question, you will need a pencil and a sheet of tracing paper. Place the tracing paper over this page. Carefully follow all the directions given below. They will lead you to the spaceship's destination. Hint: It will be easier if you rewrite the complete word at each step.

The solution is on page 124.

1. Print the word SPACESHIP. _____

2. Remove the first vowel from the right; replace it with an A. _____

3. Insert an I in the first position at the left. _____

4. Place a T after every S and every A. _____

5. Remove the third consonant from the left; replace it with an N. _____

6. Remove the last letter and replace it with an O and an E. _____

7. Remove the fifth consonant from the left and the fifth letter from the right. _____

8. Place an R in the eleventh position from the left. _____

9. Place an S in the fourth position from the right. Then insert a D before the first vowel from the left. _____

10. Locate the fifth and sixth letters from the left; reverse their order. _____

11. Move the letters from the last three positions at the right to the first three positions at the left. _____

12. Remove all the E's. _____

Teeth are one of the most common weapons that animals use for hunting and fighting.

ANIMAL WEAPONS

Any animal that hunts needs weapons to capture its food. Teeth and claws are the most common hunting weapons, but there are many others. Some animals catch their prey by poisoning them, electrocuting them, or even by shooting at them.

Animals also need weapons to fight off enemies. When a wild animal is threatened, it usually tries to escape. But if it is cornered or protecting its young, it will fight back. It may bite, scratch, stab, sting, or shock. It may bombard its enemy with hot gas, burning acid, or a smelly spray.

TEETH

Hunting animals usually have strong jaws and sharp teeth. If you look at the jaws of a dog or a cat, you will see four long pointed teeth—two in the upper jaw and two in the lower. These are called canine teeth, or fangs. Canines are the chief weapons of many hunting animals. Like daggers, they are used for stabbing and slashing.

Monkeys and apes also have long canine

teeth, but they use them mainly for self-defense. A monkey threatens an enemy by opening its mouth and flashing its dangerous canines.

Animals such as elephants, walruses, and wild pigs are armed with tusks—extra-long teeth that grow out of an animal's mouth. An African elephant will defend her helpless calf from lions and leopards by charging and stabbing with her tusks. She can kill any enemy instantly with one powerful thrust. Tusks are used for digging up food as well as for fighting.

Fish have a greater variety of teeth than any other group of animals. Since they have no limbs to help them grasp their prey, they must rely on their teeth to seize and hold whatever they catch. Some fish have teeth not only in their jaws but also on their tongues or even far back in their throats.

A shark's teeth have jagged edges and pointed tips, like steak knives. Most sharks have several rows of teeth, lined up one behind another. New teeth are growing in all the time. When the teeth in the front row are old and worn, they drop out. Then the teeth in the row behind move in to take their place. During a ten-year period, a tiger shark will grow, use, and shed as many as 24,000 teeth.

CLAWS, TALONS, AND HOOVES

A cat's claws can be as dangerous as its teeth. Lions, tigers, and all other cats use their claws to hook their prey and pull it down. Because of the way a cat's claws are curved, they make very effective weapons. Once they dig into the flesh, the victim's struggling only serves to draw them in deeper.

Except for the cheetah, all cats can pull their claws back into their toes. When a cat walks or runs, it keeps its claws pulled in so they will not be blunted by the hard ground. When it climbs or fights, it pushes its claws out.

Other animals with claws—such as dogs, bears, and raccoons—cannot pull them in. They use their claws mainly for digging or climbing rather than hunting or fighting. Even so, their claws can still cause plenty of damage. A bear fights by striking an enemy with its front paws. When it hits its target, its heavy claws can rip and tear.

Birds of prey hunt with the pointed talons on their feet. An eagle will swoop down from the sky, snatch up a rabbit with its talons, and carry it away. Some birds, such as the flightless ostrich, defend themselves with their feet. An ostrich has long muscular legs with two toes on each foot. The big toe is armed with a thick sharp nail. The ostrich fights by kicking. Its kick can be more dangerous than that of a horse.

Hoofed animals also fight by kicking. A zebra can smash an enemy's teeth with a well-aimed kick.

HORNS AND ANTLERS

Horns are used for self-defense by grazing animals like goats, sheep, cattle, and antelope. The horns of a Rocky Mountain goat are short and curved. A mother goat protecting her kid has been known to kill a bear by stabbing it in the heart. A male bighorn sheep has thick, heavy, tightly curled horns, which it uses as battering rams.

This warthog may look harmless coming out of a mudbath, but don't get too close—its tusks are deadly.

A bear attacks by striking out with its front paws. When it hits its victim, its heavy claws can rip and tear.

Male bighorns use their heavy horns as battering rams.

When a gemsbok attacks, it lowers its head so its swordlike horns are pointing at the enemy.

In Africa, an antelope called the gemsbok has horns like swords that may be four feet long. When a gemsbok attacks, it lowers its head between its legs, so the sharp tips of its horns are pointing at the enemy. A charging gemsbok can scoop up a lion with its horns and throw the lion over its back.

Antlers are found among most members of the deer family. Unlike horns, which keep on growing throughout an animal's life, antlers last only for a few months each year. They start growing in the spring, reach their full size during the winter, then drop off. The following spring, the animal grows a new set of antlers.

The pointed tips of fully grown antlers are as sharp as pitchforks. Antlers serve as weapons only during the winter mating season, when rival males fight over females. They are also used to fight off enemies such

as wolves. But once they have dropped off, the animal must rely for protection on speed and its sharp hooves.

QUILLS AND SPINES

A porcupine seems to know that it is well protected as it waddles slowly through the forest with its nose to the ground. Buried beneath its long fur are 30,000 dangerous quills that keep most enemies at a distance.

Quills are stiff hairs growing out of the porcupine's skin. They are as sharp as needles and may be five inches (12.5 centimeters) long. The pointed tip of each quill has tiny barbs, or hooks, that curve backward, like the barbs on harpoons.

Usually the quills lie flat against the porcupine's body. But when a porcupine is frightened, its quills stand on end. Twisting about on its short legs, the porcupine keeps its rear toward the enemy and whips its bristling tail back and forth. As a warning, it hisses and gnashes its teeth.

A porcupine can't shoot its quills, but it can swat an enemy with its tail. When the tail hits its target, it drives hundreds of quills into the enemy. As the victim backs away, the quills are pulled out of the porcupine and stay buried in the victim's body. Once a quill has stabbed an enemy, the barbed tip works its way into the flesh. A badly wounded animal can die of its injuries.

Some fish have spines similar to a porcupine's quills. The spines of a porcupine fish

The alarmed porcupine fish sticks out its spines in all directions, ready to stab its enemy.

resemble the prickly thorns of a rose bush. Usually, a porcupine fish swims about with its spines lying flat against its body. But when it is alarmed, it gulps water and swells up like a prickly balloon. Its spines stick out in all directions, ready to stab any enemy.

POISON

Poison is used as a weapon for hunting or self defense by many kinds of fish, snakes, and insects, as well as other animals. The poison, or venom, is produced by special glands in the animal's body. The animal injects its venom by biting or stinging.

Many fish are armed with venomous spines, which they use only for self-defense. A catfish has a sharp spine in the fin on its back and two more spines in the fins on its sides. All three spines are barbed, like a porcupine's quills. They are connected to glands that pump poison into an enemy's wounds. When a catfish is alarmed, it lifts its spines and locks them in place. It fights by twisting about in the water, jabbing at the enemy with its spines. Fishermen must handle catfish with great care to avoid being stung.

The deadliest of all venomous fish is the ugly little stonefish, found off the coast of Australia. A stonefish lies hidden among stones and debris in shallow water, waiting to leap forward and snap up its prey. Its body is covered with warts and coated with algae and slime, making it almost invisible.

Eighteen jagged spines jut out from its body. These fish are considered as deadly as cobras. Swimmers in Australia have died within an hour after stepping on a stonefish.

Venomous snakes use their poison to capture food, as well as in self-defense. They can strike and kill with lightning speed. A rattlesnake has two hollow fangs in its upper jaw. Each fang is connected to a poison gland in the rattler's cheek. When the snake sinks its fangs into a victim, its cheeks squeeze against the poison glands. Poison squirts into the wound through tiny holes in the tips of the fangs. A rattlesnake bite can kill a rabbit in a few minutes. It can also kill a person unless the victim receives quick medical aid.

The biggest venomous snakes are cobras, which live in Africa and Asia. A king cobra may be 18 feet (5.5 meters) long. A cobra

A rattlesnake has two hollow fangs connected to poison glands. Its deadly bite can kill a small animal in minutes.

warns an enemy by rearing up, hissing loudly, and spreading the skin of its neck into a wide hood. Some cobras can spit their poison through small holes in the front of their fangs. They are said to aim at the eyes of their enemies.

Spiders capture food just as some snakes do—with a poisonous bite. Like a rattlesnake, a spider has two sharp fangs connected to poison glands in its head. All spiders are poisonous, but only a few, like the black widow, are dangerous to humans. Most spiders are so small that their fangs cannot pierce human skin.

Hornets, wasps, and bees have poisonous stingers at the tips of their tails. A bee's venom is similar to a snake's, but it is not as dangerous because it is released in much smaller amounts. Some ants also have poisonous stingers in their tails, which they use to kill enemies and capture the creatures they eat. Ants can also bite with their powerful ice-tong jaws. An ant will often bite an enemy, then turn around and squirt poison into the wound.

CHEMICAL WARFARE

A skunk cannot really injure an enemy. Yet it is armed with one of nature's most effective weapons—a bad-smelling chemical spray. Most animals quickly get out of the way when they see a skunk coming.

A skunk always gives warning before it fires. It lowers its head and drums on the ground with its front paws. It may click its teeth and growl or hiss. If the enemy doesn't retreat, the skunk lifts its bushy tail. That's the last warning. Suddenly the skunk twists around into a U-shaped position. It aims its tail at the enemy and lets go with its stinking spray.

Skunk spray comes from two stink glands beneath the skunk's tail. Each gland is connected to a small tube that lies hidden under the skin. When the skunk fires, the tubes pop out like a pair of nozzles. They squirt two streams of thick, oily fluid that join together in a misty spray.

A skunk can aim straight ahead, to either side, or up into the air. It can shoot its spray about 12 feet (3.5 meters), even more if the spray is carried by the wind. The strong smell of skunk spray can make a person or animal sick. If the spray hits the eyes, they will sting and burn until tears wash the spray out.

Skunks aren't the only animals that use odor as a weapon. Snakes, weasels, minks, wolverines, and several other animals have scent glands similar to a skunk's but not as powerful.

Some insects are also equipped for chemical warfare. When they are threatened, they release a fluid or gas that stinks, burns, or stings. A stink bug drives off enemies by giving off a repulsive smell. Some ants can spray a burning acid. The bombardier beetle attacks enemies by blasting them with hot gas that shoots out from the tail end of its body.

The bombardier beetle attacks enemies by shooting hot gas from the tail end of its body.

When a hungry chameleon spots an insect, it uncoils its long, sticky-tipped tongue and hauls the victim into its mouth.

UNUSUAL WEAPONS

Fish are the only animals that have the power to shock their enemies. About 250 kinds of fish can send an electrical charge into the water. The most powerful of these is the electric eel, which lives in South American rivers.

In the eel's tail are bundles of special cells that produce electricity in much the same way as an electric battery. As the eel swims along, it gives off a weak current that helps it find its way in muddy river waters. When it finds food or is alarmed, it can deliver an electric shock of up to 650 volts. That's enough power to stun the fish and frogs it feeds on and to jolt enemies like alligators.

Frogs and toads use their long sticky tongues as hunting weapons. They catch insects by flicking out their tongues. The champion tongue-flicker, however, is a reptile, the African chameleon. Usually, a chameleon's tongue is folded up inside its mouth. When it spots an insect, it creeps forward, takes aim, opens its mouth, and fires. Its tongue, longer than its body, shoots out like a spring uncoiling. The swollen tip of the tongue is coated with a sticky fluid that can trap big insects as well as small reptiles and birds. After hitting its target, the chameleon hauls its meal back into its mouth.

Of all the animals that use weapons, the archerfish is in a class by itself. It shoots water bullets at its prey. These little fish live in Australia and Southeast Asia. They hunt by waiting below the surface of a pond, with the tips of their mouths sticking out of the water. When an archerfish sees an insect or spider on a leaf or plant stem, it closes its gills and forces water into its mouth. Then it presses its tongue against the roof of its mouth and fires droplets of water in a rapid stream.

An archerfish can score a bull's-eye from several feet away. The fast jet of water knocks the insect or spider off its perch. It falls into the pond, where it is seized and swallowed by the sharpshooting archerfish.

Few animals have a weapon as unusual as that of the archerfish. But every animal uses the weapons it was born with—to hunt and to protect itself—so it can stay alive for another day.

RUSSELL FREEDMAN
Author, *Tooth and Claw*

95

GET LOST!

You might wonder why anyone would think that getting lost is fun. But getting lost—and finding your way again—is the whole idea behind a maze.

A maze, or labyrinth, is an intricate pattern of passages. It can be a drawing, or it can be something you actually walk through. The goal is to find your way through the passages and come out again. But wrong turns and dead ends fool you all along the way.

People have been fascinated by mazes since ancient times. The Egyptians and the Greeks built underground mazes that may have been used to store treasure (and befuddle any would-be thieves). Some of these mazes may have been prisons. But whatever their actual use, mazes played an important role in the myths of the ancient world.

The most famous mythological maze was the labyrinth of Crete. Legend says that Daedalus, the master craftsman, built the labyrinth for King Minos of Crete. In the labyrinth Minos confined the Minotaur, a half-man, half-bull monster who devoured anyone who entered. And no one who entered ever came out—until Theseus, the legendary hero of Athens, arrived. Theseus unrolled a spool of thread behind him as he went deep into the labyrinth. Then he slew the Minotaur and followed the thread to find his way out.

In Europe during the Middle Ages, maze patterns were built into the tiled floors of churches and cathedrals. These mazes may have symbolized the difficult path of a Christian pilgrimage. Mazes were also carved into the earth of village greens, just for fun.

Mazes became a favorite amusement of European royalty and nobility. Nobles often planted hedges in the form of mazes in their gardens. Many hedge gardens were planted in geometric patterns that were not at all hard to walk through. But others were truly confusing.

One of the best-known hedge mazes was planted in the late 1600's at Hampton Court, near London, by the English King William

The labyrinth of Crete, the most famous mythological maze, as imagined by an 18th-century artist.

III. There the members of the court held races to see who could find the way to the center of the maze and back in the fastest time. Today this maze still confuses and delights visitors to Hampton Court.

What may be the most complicated hedge maze anywhere opened in 1978 at Longleat, one of Britain's most famous estates. The Longleat maze covers an area larger than a football field. More than 16,000 waist-high yew trees were planted to form it. As the trees grow to form a towering hedge, the Longleat maze will become the most impenetrable in the world.

It's already confusing enough. The maze has two parts. The first section can be figured out in about half an hour. But the challenging second part will keep the daring befuddled for a much longer time. Six bridges add to the confusion. And the maze's four resting spots have been designed to look exactly alike. Coming on one, you're certain you've passed that way before . . . or have you?

The Longleat maze in Britain, which opened in 1978, may be the most complicated hedge maze in the world.

MARBLEOUS MARBLES

There is a little world in which you'll find some odd creatures —*aggies, commies, puries, immies, steelies,* and *glassies*. There may also be some *alleys,* and if you're lucky, you may even see a *black beauty.* Into this little world steps a *mibster,* who shoots a *taw,* hoping for a *stick.* A stick means that the mibster may shoot again!

What little world has such creatures in it? Can you guess? It's the world of marbles, a game that has been played for centuries in many different countries and in many different ways. Marbles —those tiny, smooth spheres of glass or stone or steel—are delightful to play with, to look at, and to hold.

Have you ever stuck your hand into a bag of marbles and grabbed a bunch? They are smooth and round and cool to the touch. When you shake a couple in your closed palm, they rattle around with pleasing clicks.

Some marbles may be as small as peas, others as large as golf balls. But most are middle-sized, about as big as a sour ball candy. Glassies—glass marbles—may be clear or opaque. A purie is clear (pure) glass, without a pattern running through it. Aggies are made of polished agate, or they may be made of marble or limestone. Commies are small marbles that are shot at in various marbles games. Immies get their name from the fact that they are imitation aggies, made of glazed or fired clay. An immie may be used as a commie.

Steelies are usually ball bearings. They are often quite heavy because they are made from steel, iron, or brass. Alleys are made of alabaster. Of all these different types of marbles, aggies are thought to be the best, though some people prefer alleys, and a shining purie is lovely indeed. But above all, a collector of marbles will cherish a black beauty. It's a heavy marble, usually made of black agate or obsidian. Black beauties, like priceless gems, are quite rare.

MIBSTERS, TAWS, AND STICKS

Ancient peoples played with marbles. They used sheep's knucklebones, small stones, polished wood, and even tiny nuts. Some of these types of marbles exist today in various countries around the world.

There are many different ways to play with marbles, and the game has many different names. In the United States it's called Marbles or Immies or Mibs. English, Irish, and Scottish youngsters play Boss or Taw or Span. In Africa it is Jorrah, and in Brazil it is Gude. Call it what you will, any mibster (marble-player) would surely agree that the game is a lot of fun.

Although there are many variations, there are only three basic ways in which the game is played.

1. Hole games, in which marbles are shot into, out of, or near holes in the ground or in boxes.

2. Chase games, in which players shoot their marbles at opponents' marbles as they follow a winding course.

3. Enclosure games, in which players shoot their marbles at other marbles within an enclosure such as a circle or a square.

A popular enclosure game is Ringer. In Ringer, 13 marbles are placed in the shape of a cross in the middle of a 10-foot (3-meter) circle. If you are the mibster, you take your shooting marble (called a shooter or taw), and you try to knock each of the commies (target marbles) out of the circle (ring). When your taw stays inside the ring, that is called a stick, and you shoot again. But if you miss, it's your opponent's turn. The mibster who knocks out the most marbles is the winner.

The key to winning is in the shooting. There's a special way to hold your shooter for best results. The shooter should be nestled inside the crook of your index finger. But some champions insist that it's better to have the marble resting between the index finger and the second finger, right at the first joints. Hold the shooter there tightly with your full thumb nail pressing against it. When you flick your thumb, the marble shoots out. It sounds easy, but it's difficult to do well, especially when you're trying to hit another marble with your shooter. It takes practice. And in a game like Ringer, you have to learn how to put spin on your shooter so that it stays (sticks) in the ring after it knocks the commie out. If it doesn't stick, you lose your turn. Without spin, you can't win.

THE NATIONAL MARBLES TOURNAMENT

Every June, in Wildwood-by-the-Sea, New Jersey, the National Marbles Tournament is held for mibsters aged 8 to 14. About 60 boys and girls gather for the event. Most

Joelle Guiles, 14, was the girls' champ of the 1981 National Marbles Tournament.

A MARBLES GLOSSARY

Aggies, glassies, puries, alleys, immies, and **steelies**—Various types of marbles.

Black beauty—An extremely rare, heavy marble, usually made of black agate or obsidian.

Ringer—One of many marbles games. Ringer is played every year at the National Marbles Tournament.

Shooter—A marble used for shooting, usually an aggie or a glassie. Also called a **taw.**

Mibs—Target marbles. Also called **commies.**

Mibster—A marbles player.

Stick—A stick occurs when a mibster's shooter stays inside the ring after knocking a mib out of the ring. The mibster gets the chance to shoot again.

are state and regional champions. During a week of furious Ringer competition, each contestant plays some 80 games, until a girls' national champion and a boys' national champion are finally crowned.

The tournament began in 1922, and it is now sponsored by the children's television program "Big Blue Marble." (The name of the show comes from the idea that Earth, viewed from a rocket ship several thousand miles up, looks like a beautiful, big blue marble.)

In 1981, the girls' champ was 14-year-old Joelle Guiles, from Pennsylvania. The boys'

winner was 13-year-old Jeff Kimmell, from Maryland. Each won a $500 college scholarship. But neither mibster will be back in 1982. Champions are not allowed to repeat. New marbles champs will be crowned!

WHAT OTHER USES DO MARBLES HAVE?

Not all marbles games involve rolling, shooting, or throwing. Chinese Checkers is a game in which marbles are the pieces. They are moved from hole to hole on a board as each player tries to outwit the others.

And marbles are not only used in games. Have you ever picked up an aerosol can and heard something clicking inside? It's a marble. The marble is used to agitate the contents of the can. This helps the contents come out more easily when you press the button.

In the printing industry, marbles are used to make a smooth finish on copper engraving plates.

In fish hatcheries, you will see marbles on the bottom of spawning pools. They help increase the number of fish eggs that are laid.

If you are ever in an automobile at night, you will probably see a roadside sign reflect the glare of your headlights. What is doing the reflecting? Marbles, which have been inserted in the sign.

And sometimes marbles are just collected —simply because they're beautiful.

AND THE SLEEPY

HOURS OF NIGHT

THE DAY BEGINS

ARE OVER

MASQUERADE

Within the pages of this book there is a story told
Of love, adventures, fortunes lost, and a jewel of solid gold.
To solve the hidden riddle, you must use your eyes,
And find the hare in every picture that may point you to the prize.

This verse introduces *Masquerade*—a story, a series of puzzles, and a guide to buried treasure. The story tells of Jack Hare's mission to bring a beautiful jewel from Lady Moon to her love, the Sun. Jack's many adventures take him through earth, air, fire, and water. But when he finally reaches the Sun, he discovers that he has lost the precious treasure. If you can figure out all the clues (riddles, puzzles, and especially the pictures), you will know where Jack lost the jewel. You may also be lucky enough to find a *real* treasure.

For there *is* a real treasure, buried somewhere in Britain. The author of *Masquerade,* an artist named Kit Williams, made a golden figure of a hare, adorned with precious stones. He put the jewel in a hare-shaped, ceramic container and buried it—on a night of the full moon, of course. Anyone who deciphers the clues in the story and finds the jewel can have it. So can anyone outside Britain who sends the correct solution to the author. Williams has said that a child of 10 could solve the puzzle as easily as a college graduate and that no knowledge of British geography is required. People have been digging all over Britain. So read carefully—the jewel "lies waiting safe . . . for you or Eternity."

BAO LUCK FOR LUCKY

"Aw, that was just a movie," said Lucky with a shrug. He stashed the object under a bush and joined his brothers in the kitchen for a snack.

When Lucky bounded through the door, Nanny greeted him with a frown. "You naughty pup," she scolded, wagging her finger at him. "You've been digging again. Just look at your dirty paws."

So while everyone else ate biscuits and lapped milk, Lucky got a bath and a lecture.

Nanny was still toweling him dry when he heard the sounds of "The Thunderbolt Show," which was drifting into the kitchen from the living-room television set.

"Stop fidgeting," ordered Nanny, rubbing him hard with the towel. Lucky couldn't help wiggling as he heard his brothers and sisters cheering for Thunderbolt the Wonder Dog.

Dirt flew in all directions as Lucky plunged deeper into the hole he was digging.

"It's time for our snack," chorused two puppy voices.

Lucky's head popped up to see his brothers, Rolly and Patch, watching him.

"I've almost got it," he cried, and dived back into the hole. When he came up again, something dangled from his mouth. He gave it a few quick shakes and dropped it at Patch's feet.

"There!" he said proudly. "What do you think of it?"

"What is it?" asked Patch as he sniffed at it.

"I don't know, but I think it's gold. And it's real old."

Rolly looked at it closely. "It's got writing on it," he noticed. "Maybe it's an ancient relic and the writing is an evil spell—like in that movie we saw on television, *The Egyptian Ring*. Remember? The king who owned the ring had horrible things happen to him!"

A few final rubs and Nanny put Lucky down on the kitchen floor. He took off like a shot, not wanting to miss one more minute of his favorite show. Down the hall he went, and skidded around the corner into the living room. His paws dug at the carpet, but Lucky couldn't stop his skid. He hit a table leg with a dull thud. Then came a loud crash.

When Nanny rounded the corner, she found Lucky sitting among the broken remains of a flower vase.

"Lucky!" she cried. "You know you mustn't run in the house!" And Nanny carried him back to the kitchen and plopped him down in a corner.

Lucky moped in the kitchen while his brothers and sisters watched the television show. When it was over, Patch and Rolly joined him.

"I told you that thing you found had an evil spell on it," said Rolly. "Look at all the trouble you've been in today."

"What are you going to do?" asked Patch.

Lucky had had the whole "Thunderbolt" show to think about it. "I'm going to bury it again—somewhere else," he said firmly. "Then maybe the bad luck will leave me."

"We can bury it in the park tonight," suggested Rolly. "That should be far enough away."

That night, when everyone was asleep, the three pups slipped quietly out the back door. The moon was just a sliver in the sky, and a gentle breeze rustled the trees as they took turns digging a hole under the fence in the yard.

Lucky was the first to squeeze through, holding the relic gingerly between his teeth. Patch followed, calling back to Rolly, "Hurry! It's getting late."

He was answered by a yelp. "I can't get through," cried Rolly. His head was on one side of the fence, but his chubby body was on the other.

"We haven't got time to dig a deeper hole," said Patch, turning toward the park. "You'll have to stay here."

Rolly inched back into the yard and sat down. He peered through the iron fence as Patch and Lucky disappeared down the street.

By the time Lucky and Patch reached the park, the tiny moon had disappeared behind a passing cloud, and the trees lining the path loomed dark against a darker sky.

"The park sure looks different at night," said Patch with a shudder. They both quickened their steps.

It didn't take Lucky long to find a clear space near the path. Patch stood guard while Lucky scratched a shallow hole and dropped the relic into it. He was about to cover it over when Patch growled in a low voice, "I hear footsteps."

Lucky sat up, ears forward, listening. "I hear them, too," he whispered. "And they're not coming down the path. They're coming through the bushes."

Both pups peered at the bushes, but all they could see was a black tangle of branches that formed strange shapes. The footsteps came closer.

"I'm afraid," whispered Patch in a trembling voice.

Lucky was, too, but he summoned his courage and barked, "Who's there?"

No one answered. Then the footsteps began moving faster. Lucky could hear the branches snap as whatever it was moved toward them. It sounded large and horrible.

"It's the Egyptian spell!" groaned Patch, who was backing down the path. The bushes began to shake, moving back and forth, and a small white shadow leaped out onto the path.

"Boy, am I glad to see you guys!" panted Rolly. "I finally got through the fence, but then I got lost in the park. If you hadn't barked, Lucky, I would never have found you and Patch."

Then Rolly noticed how quiet his brothers were. "What's the matter?" he asked. "You look like you've seen a ghost."

"Never mind," said Lucky. "Let's get out of here." And they all ran for home.

The next afternoon, when "Thunderbolt" was over, Roger and Anita took Pongo, Perdita, and the puppies for a walk in the park —all except Lucky, Patch, and Rolly, who were curled up sleeping soundly in front of the silent television set.

Lucky was dreaming about ancient relics and angry Egyptian priests when he awoke with a start. Roger had burst through the door, followed by the rest of the family.

"Nanny!" he called out. "Look what Pongo found in the park."

Lucky was horrified to see Roger holding up the relic he had buried in the park. Now Pongo would have bad luck!

"What on earth is that?" Nanny asked, taking the object from Roger and turning it over carefully in her hand.

"It's a medal of valor that belonged to my father," said Roger in an excited voice. "The one I thought Pongo had buried in the backyard when he was a pup."

Roger reached down and gave Pongo a pat on the head. "I still can't imagine what it was doing in the park," he said, scratching his head. "Oh, well. I have it back again. This must be my lucky day."

"Mine, too," thought Lucky. And he breathed a sigh of relief.

Slide to the ground . . .

Climb up the outside . . .

FANTASY PLAYHOUSES

Imagine all the wonderful things you could do in one of these playhouses. Play a game of hide-and-seek. Act out an adventure story. Dance. Climb. Sit and daydream.

Does one of the playhouses remind you of a castle? If so, be its king or queen. Is one like a spaceship? Be an astronaut headed for distant stars. Is one a ship? Be its captain, guiding it through a stormy sea.

These playhouses were created by artists who wanted to give children places in which to use their imaginations. Children even helped to build some of the playhouses. They mixed concrete, dug holes, hammered nails, and painted. And they gave their ideas on how to design the structures.

Even before the playhouses were completed, children were using them. They knew that they had a play place—and a fantasy world—of their own.

Hide under the stairs .

POPULAR CRAFTS

The trend to "make-it-yourself" continued to grow in 1981. More and more people valued handmade items over manufactured ones. And people who had never before tried their hands at a craft eagerly completed one project after another. They discovered that crafts give us a chance to express ourselves with our hands and imaginations. And crafts are an exciting way to spend leisure time.

Do you have a favorite craft? Perhaps some of the following projects will appeal to you. Some are easy, some are hard. But each one will give a feeling of satisfaction at having created something both attractive and useful.

CLOISONNÉ

Cloisonné is a type of enamel work. On a metal backing, areas are partitioned off by thin strips of wire, forming a design. The areas between the wires—called *cloisons,* the French word for compartments—are filled with layers of finely ground glass enamels. After each layer is applied, the piece is fired (baked in a special oven called a kiln). The layers are applied until the enamel is flush with the tops of the wires. One sim-

ple piece may be fired as many as twenty times before it is completed.

Cloisonné is an art craft that demands great precision and patience. In ancient times, it was used to decorate jewelry, sculpture, bowls, vases, and religious articles. Today the technique is used mainly on jewelry. The metal backings are usually copper, brass, silver, and gold. The glass enamels come in a great variety of colors.

Cloisonné is a type of enamel work that is today used mainly on jewelry.

Folk painting can be used on a wide variety of wooden and metal objects.

FOLK PAINTING

Folk painting is a form of decoration that draws on interesting and unusual techniques from the past. It can be used on a wide variety of wooden and metal objects—trunks, plaques, trays, milk cans, cutting boards, and furniture. You can paint on new objects, or you can search attics, flea markets, and barns for old ones.

The designs that can be painted are almost endless. Try landscapes, fruits, flowers, portraits, or figures. And there are several techniques to choose from—stenciling, freehand, and traditional styles from other countries. For example, *rosemaling* ("rose painting") is a Norwegian peasant style that uses freehand floral designs. It is used on furniture and accessories and even on the walls of homes.

Folk painting is fairly easy to master. You need only learn the basic brushstrokes and coloring techniques. And since stencil patterns are often used, strong drawing talent is not essential.

111

A sock monkey is adorable. And if you add a bit of Velcro to the hands, it can perform some amusing tricks.

You can make beautiful silk flowers, "string" them, and wear them like a festive lei.

SOCK MONKEYS

Adorable monkeys can be made from a special kind of men's work socks—they are gray and white with a red wedge woven into the heel. The socks are cut out according to a pattern and then stuffed with fiberfill to make the monkey bodies. The monkeys come to life with a few extra touches—button eyes, an embroidered nose and mouth, a little scarf or bow tie. And if some Velcro is attached to the hands, your sock monkey will be able to perform some amusing tricks.

SILK FLOWERS

Beautiful silk or organdy flowers can be made in any season. They can be "strung" and worn like a festive lei. Or wire stems can be added to make a flower arrangement for your home. Put one on a special gift, or wear one in your hair.

Twelve petals are in each flower, and they are cut from a pattern. The petals are folded

These incredibly real-looking bread dough flowers *(above)* were made from a mixture of white bread and glue *(below)*.

and wired together and then fastened around pearled stamens. If you use white silk, you can dye the petals with batik dyes. Silk leaves can be bought, or you can cut them out from a piece of green silk.

BREAD DOUGH FLOWERS

Flowers can also be made from bread. By mixing measured amounts of white glue and fresh white bread, you will get a non-sticky, easy-to-shape dough that can be colored with acrylic paint or food coloring. The dough is then rolled and squeezed into petals, and the petals are overlapped to form flowers. Wire stems covered with green tape are inserted, and the flowers are dried at room temperature.

Bread dough flowers look incredibly real, and they last for years. Try making a vase of yellow roses for your mother.

WENDIE R. BLANCHARD
Managing Editor
Creative Crafts magazine

113

The armadillo gets its name from its armorlike covering. Some armadillos have hairs that are so long that the armor is nearly hidden.

A PIG IN TURTLE'S CLOTHING

Feel sorry for the poor armadillo. People laugh at it and make jokes about it. They poke fun at the way it looks. Some people liken it to an army tank. Others say it has the face of a mouse and the ears of a donkey. The famous naturalist John James Audubon said it looked like "a small pig with the shell of a turtle."

THE LITTLE ARMORED ONE

There are about 20 species, or kinds, of armadillos. They are found throughout South and Central America. One species, the nine-banded armadillo, has extended its range into the southern part of the United States.

The smallest armadillo, the pichiciago, is only 6 inches (15 centimeters) long. The largest species, the giant armadillo, is up to 40 inches (100 centimeters) long—not counting its tail, which may be 20 inches (50 centimeters) long. The nine-banded armadillo is about 2 feet (60 centimeters) long, including its tail, and weighs about 14 pounds (6.5 kilograms)—it's a little larger than a house cat. It is brown speckled, with a shell over its back and its long tail.

Armadillos are usually classified in a group of mammals called edentates, or "toothless ones." Actually, armadillos have lots of teeth. One kind, the giant armadillo, has more than 90 teeth. But armadillo teeth are small, without true roots, and are more or less useless. The animal's main eating tool is its long sticky tongue.

The armadillo received its name from early Spanish explorers of the New World. The name, which translates into English as "little armored one," refers to the armorlike covering that protects the animal.

This armor consists of a series of strong, bony plates within the skin. The plates cover the back and in some cases the head and the tail of the animal. The plates are connected by flexible skin, which enables the armadillo to bend its body. Between the plates grow hard, brushlike hairs. Some kinds of armadillos have hairs that are so long and thick that they nearly hide the armor.

The undersides of the armadillo are not protected by armor. Most kinds of armadillos can roll up into a ball when they are attacked. This protects their tender undersides. Only the armor is exposed, and many of the armadillos' enemies cannot bite through it.

An armadillo has four short legs, ending in clawed feet. The middle toes on its front feet are long and heavy. These are toes used for digging.

Armadillos are surprisingly fast runners. They can run faster than people and faster than most dogs. As soon as it thinks it has outdistanced its pursuer, an armadillo quickly digs into the ground. In two minutes it can disappear from view—even in soil so hard that a person would need a pickaxe to crack it. Once underground, the armadillo uses its feet and armor to anchor itself. This makes it almost impossible to pull an armadillo out of the ground.

An armadillo can hold its breath for up to ten minutes. Thus a stream or river presents no barrier to this animal. If the stream is narrow, the animal holds its breath and walks along the bottom, under water. If the stream is wide, the armadillo inflates itself. It takes a big gulp of air before entering the water. This helps keep it afloat as it swims along the surface, with only its snout showing above the water.

Armadillos feed mainly on insects, particularly ants, termites, grasshoppers, and other destructive pests. They also eat scorpions, tarantulas, and, occasionally, snakes, mice, berries, and dead animals. In their search for food they may uproot young plants, an activity not appreciated by farmers and gardeners.

When not out looking for food, the armadillo lives in its burrow, which it may share with other armadillos or even with rabbits or a rattlesnake. The burrow usually has a long corridor that opens into a large chamber that the armadillo lines with leaves or grass.

The burrow is where a female gives birth to her young. An armadillo mother gives birth to four babies at a time—and they are all exactly alike. The mother may have four identical girls or four identical boys. Or perhaps she has "twins"—eight identical babies all of the same sex. The babies are pink and have soft shell plates. Within two weeks the armor hardens, and the babies leave their mother to live on their own.

In the 1970's, scientists discovered an unusual fact about armadillos: They catch human leprosy. This disease, which is caused by a bacterium, affects the skin and nerve tissues of humans. Armadillos are one of only two types of mammals known to contract human leprosy. Scientists are conducting research on armadillos in an effort to learn more about the disease.

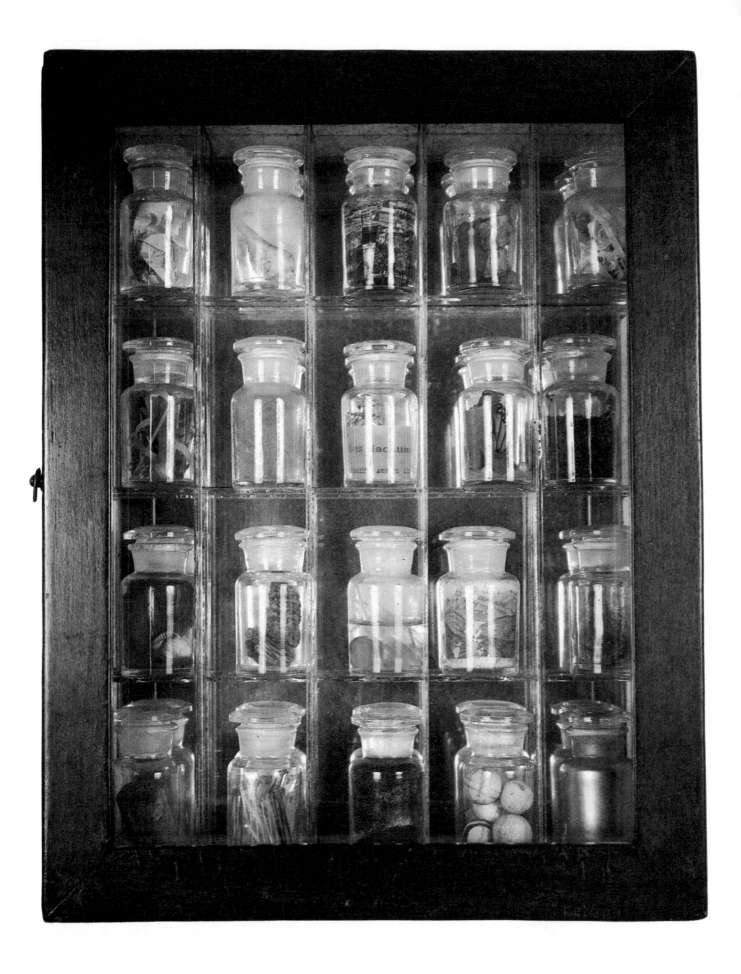

JOSEPH CORNELL'S MAGICAL BOXES

Joseph Cornell was an artist who lived in two worlds. One was the ordinary, everyday world in which we all live. The other was a magical world that existed only in his imagination. But because of his creations, all of us can see his magical world.

Cornell constructed hundreds of small wood boxes. He filled these boxes with familiar objects—seashells, marbles, twigs, cutouts of people and animals, clock springs, bird feathers. His magic lies in the unique way he selected and arranged these common objects. Cornell was able to make each box a little dreamworld of delight and mystery.

COLLECTING "LOOT"

Cornell was born in 1903. For most of his life he lived in Flushing, an area of New York City. He would travel by subway into Manhattan, where he would spend many hours looking for materials for his boxes. He visited old bookshops, record stores, souvenir shops, and five-and-dime stores. He collected all sorts of "loot," as he called it. Postage stamps, photographs, ballet programs, magazines, driftwood, sequins, clay pipes, toys, and coins were found and saved.

None of these cost a lot of money. Cornell couldn't afford to buy expensive things. But although they were inexpensive, Cornell thought of them as treasures. They were the raw materials of his work.

It took Cornell a long time to make one of his boxes. He wanted to create a feeling of age. He polished the wood so that it would look old. If the wood was painted, he might put it in the oven. The heat would make the paint peel and crack. Sometimes he would paste pages from old books and magazines on the back of a box.

Tilly Losch

Opposite page: *Pharmacy*

The Hotel Eden

The most time-consuming part was arranging his treasures in the box. This could take weeks. Cornell moved things around and added or removed items, until he felt "a sense of rightness."

Each of the objects in a box had a special meaning—it was a symbol. A seashell was a symbol of the sea. A feather on the floor of a box symbolized a bird that had flown away. A spiral watch spring symbolized time.

Often, Cornell's works showed unexpected connections between very different objects. He showed the similarity between the seams in a ship's sails and the threads of a spider's web. He showed connections between soap bubbles and planets, and between butterflies and ballerinas.

Cornell died in 1972, but his work lives on. His magical boxes are exhibited all over the world, enchanting people everywhere.

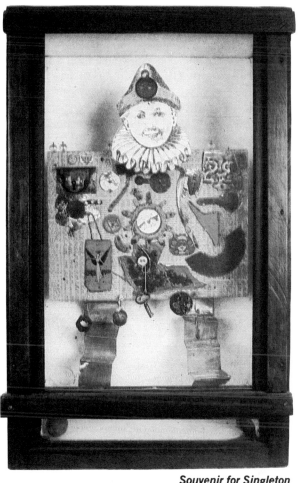

Souvenir for Singleton

Medici Princess

Paul and Virginia

THE SKATING BOOM

Figure skating has been around since the 1700's. But only in recent years has it become a ''hot'' sport in North America. If people aren't watching it on TV or going to live ice shows, they're out on the ice themselves. Why has figure skating suddenly become so popular?

Much of the new interest has to do with television. During the 1960's and 1970's, people were able to watch the Winter Olympics right in their own living rooms. They saw the beauty and theatrics of figure skating and the skill and grace of the competitors. In time, the world and national championships, skating exhibitions, and ice shows were televised. People saw different techniques and more complicated routines. And the more people learned about figure skating, the more fascinated they were by the sport.

The individual skating styles and personalities of the young competitors added to the new wave of interest. Names like Peggy Fleming, Dorothy Hamill, John Curry, Tai Babilonia, and Randy Gardner were recognized by almost everyone, and fans avidly followed the careers of their favorites.

In 1981, several new skaters attracted the public's attention—among them, Elaine Zayak and Peter and Caitlin Carruthers.

Elaine Zayak. Fifteen-year-old Elaine Zayak, from Paramus, New Jersey, won the 1981 U.S. women's figure-skating championship. Not only did she win, but she stunned the world by doing something that no other female skater had ever done before in competition: She made seven triple-revolution jumps during a four-minute routine. In a triple jump, the skater leaps up from the ice and whirls around three times in the air before touching down on the ice again.

Just a month after the U.S. championships, Elaine placed second in the world championships, winning the silver medal. Once again, she completed seven triple jumps. But she also became the center of a controversy.

Figure skating is partly an athletic sport and partly a graceful art form because its

Elaine Zayak

Caitlin and Peter Carruthers

movements are a lot like ballet. There have always been some acrobatic routines in figure skating, but nothing as daring as Elaine's jumps. Some critics say that Elaine's style doesn't have enough grace. They worry that she may begin a trend in which women's figure skating will lose its dancelike qualities and become too acrobatic. But Elaine has said, "People have said what I do isn't figure skating, but they're into ballet. I think the sport is changing, becoming more athletic. I think people like my way better."

Elaine's "way" has been developing since she was about 4 years old, when she began to skate. Then her parents bought a trampoline, and she learned to jump. Elaine put these two skills together and has become the "jumpingest" figure skater ever known. And in case anyone has any doubts, Elaine has announced that she wants to be the next Olympic champ. It's certain that her fans will be rooting for her at the 1984 Winter Olympics, at Sarajevo, Yugoslavia.

Peter and Caitlin Carruthers. Twenty-one-year-old Peter and 19-year-old Caitlin also excelled at the 1981 U.S. figure-skating championships: They won the gold in the pairs event.

They suffered a setback just a short time later, when they placed only fifth in the world championships. But they skate so well together that many experts feel they will become a top twosome in the sport.

Pairs skating involves a team of a man and a woman. The style is athletic, rather than acrobatic or balletic. Pairs skating involves something else, too—a special relationship, a special closeness, between the partners. They must think and act in the same way.

Peter and Caitlin (or Kitty, as she is often called) certainly have that special relationship. They are brother and sister, although not by birth—as babies they were adopted into the same family. They grew up in Burlington, Massachusetts. When their father built a backyard ice rink, Peter played hockey, and Caitlin skated. Peter then switched to figure skating, and from then on, they worked together and developed the energetic style of figure skating that they have become known for.

Their hard work began to pay off when they skated to fifth place in the 1980 Winter Olympics. And they, like Elaine Zayak, are looking forward to skating to first at the 1984 Games.

INDEX

ILLUSTRATION CREDITS AND ACKNOWLEDGMENTS

14– Artist, Michèle A.
19 McLean
20– James J. C. Andrews
21
22 Rita Ford Music Boxes
23 Joseph B. Brignolo, Jr.,
    from the collection of
    Gerald Planus
24 Joseph B. Brignolo, Jr.,
    from the collection of
    Gerald Planus; Rita Ford
    Music Boxes
25 Joseph B. Brignolo, Jr.,
    from the collection of
    Gerald Planus
26– Artist, Michèle A.
27 McLean
28 Owen Flipschulke—
    Black Star
29 NASA
30 Artist, Frank Senyk;
    Brian Sullivan—*Discover*
    magazine ©1981 Time, Inc.
31 Artist, Frank Senyk;
    Brian Sullivan—*Discover*
    magazine ©1981 Time, Inc.
32– *Soviet Life* magazine
33
38– Jenny Tesar
40
41 Marv Poulson
42 The Bettmann Archive
43 George Ortiz Collection,
    courtesy the Art Institute
    of Chicago; Archaeological
    Museum of Thessalonike,
    courtesy the Art Institute
    of Chicago; Pella Museum,
    courtesy the Art Institute
    of Chicago
44– Archaeological Museum
45 of Thessalonike, courtesy
    the Art Institute of
    Chicago
46 Bill Meng—New York
    Zoological Society
47 Dennis De Mello—New
    York Zoological Society

48 ©Porterfield Chickering—
    Photo Researchers
49– Artwork from *See Inside*
51 *a Castle* ©Grisewood &
    Dempsey Ltd., London
53 ©1979 Frederick Ayer—
    Photo Researchers
54 Orion Press
55 Alan Clifton—Black Star
56– Artist, Dale Barsanian
57
62 Courtesy Franklin
    Institute
64 ©1981 Black Star
65 Snowdon—Camera Press
66 Camera Press
67 Snowdon—Camera Press
68– Kjell B. Sandved
69
71 Artist, Michèle A.
    McLean
72 Harold E. Edgerton;
    Charles E. Miller
73 Zimmerman—FPG;
    Harold E. Edgerton
74– Harold E. Edgerton
75
76– Peter D. Capen
77
78– Courtesy of Scholastic
81 Photography Awards,
    conducted by Scholastic
    Magazines, Inc. and
    sponsored by Eastman
    Kodak Company
86– Jenny Tesar
88
89 Solution: To Distant
    Stars
90 Jane Burton—Bruce
    Coleman, Inc.
91 Clem Haagner—Bruce
    Coleman, Inc.; Robert L.
    Dunne; Bob & Clara
    Calhoun—Bruce
    Coleman, Inc.
92 ©Keith Gunnar—Bruce
    Coleman, Inc.

93 Jane Burton—Bruce
    Coleman, Inc.; Tom
    McHugh—Photo
    Researchers
94 ©Charles E. Mohr—
    NAS/Photo Researchers
95 Kim Taylor—Bruce
    Coleman, Inc.
96 The Bettmann Archive
97 ©Georg Gerster—Photo
    Researchers
98 Jenny Tesar
100 Dan Farrell
102– Photos reprinted by
103 permission of Schocken
    Books, Inc., from
    Masquerade by Kit
    Williams, ©1979 by Kit
    Williams
108 Emily de Rham; Betty
    Klavun
109 Betty Klavun
110– Courtesy *Creative Crafts*
113 magazine
114 ©C. Haagner—Bruce
    Coleman, Inc.; N. Myers
    —Bruce Coleman, Inc.
116 Collection Mrs. Marcel
    Duchamp, Paris, photo
    by Jacques Faujour
117 Collection Mr. and Mrs.
    E. A. Bergman, Chicago
118 National Gallery of
    Canada
119 ©Estate of Joseph
    Cornell, courtesy Castelli
    Feigen Corcoran Gallery,
    New York; Private
    Collection, photo by Kate
    Keller; Collection Mr.
    and Mrs. E. A. Bergman,
    Chicago
120 Diana Di Giacomo—
    Focus on Sports
121 Focus on Sports